Back to Hope

A MEMOIR ABOUT FINDING MEANING AND HEALING THROUGH SURRENDER

DR. KAREN HYDEN

Contents

Foreword vii
A Letter to the Reader ix

1. The Early Years That Shaped Me 1
2. A Move and a Family Fractured 13
3. Adolescence and the Pressure to be Perfect 21
4. Nothing Left but a Surrender 31
5. Gaining Confidence 43
6. Learning the Realities of Love and Life 51
7. First Heartbreak 61
8. New Beginnings 65
9. A Rocky Start 75
10. Transitions 83
11. My Love Story is Not My Whole Story 91
12. The Aftermath of Betrayal 97
13. Spiritual Warfare 103
14. Two Hearts Redeemed 111
15. Seeds Planted, a Life in Bloom 121
16. Lyme Disease and Deeper Healing 135
17. The Launch 147

Afterword 157
Acknowledgments 161
About the Author 163
Also from Dr. Karen Hyden 165

Copyright © 2024 Karen Hyden

All rights reserved.

No part of this book may be reproduced in any form or by any electronic or mechanical means, including information storage and retrieval systems, without written permission from the author, except for the use of brief quotations in a book review.

All Scripture quotations, unless otherwise indicated, are taken from the Holy Bible, New International Version®, NIV®. Copyright ©1973, 1978, 1984, 2011 by Biblica, Inc.™ Used by permission of Zondervan. All rights reserved worldwide. www.zondervan.com The "NIV" and "New International Version" are trademarks registered in the United States Patent and Trademark Office by Biblica, Inc.™

Scripture quotations marked (NLT) are taken from the *Holy Bible*, New Living Translation, copyright ©1996, 2004, 2015 by Tyndale House Foundation. Used by permission of Tyndale House Publishers, Carol Stream, Illinois 60188. All rights reserved.

Book Cover Design: Dee Dee Book Covers
Author Photo Credit: Joaquin Films Co.

Paperback: 978-1-964924-01-4
Hardcover: 978-1-964924-02-1
Ebook: 978-1-964924-03-8

To the reader who is opening this book feeling hopeless, lost, stuck, or forgotten: May you experience a renewed sense of hope and purpose as you see yourself reflected in my story and realize how faithfully the Lord has been working in yours.

Foreword

I LOVE a good story, and I know you do, too! So, settle into your comfy chair with this book by my thoughtful and selfless friend, Karen Hyden. *Back to Hope* almost turns the pages by itself, and you surely won't want it to end.

Karen is a magnificent woman of faith, and from the moment I met her, I knew we would stay connected. God brought a beautiful friend into my life, a woman with a unique perspective and a heart for helping others on their own journey to healing. I'm so thankful she chose to share her story with us in such a vulnerable and authentic way.

As you read this treasure, let her journey inspire you. Karen has reflected deeply on life's twists and turns, seeing God's hand in every obstacle and every test. She explores how God is always at work in our lives, in both the "big and little things." Sometimes, in the chaos, it's hard to see His plan, but Karen shows us that hindsight often reveals His purpose.

We can see the tests that God has placed before us, the discipline He provided so that we could be more like Jesus, the guidance He provided just when we might have strayed,

FOREWORD

and even the love He lavished upon us when we needed it most. The ultimate Potter, God molds us into the vessel He has planned for us to be all along.

We might not always see it in the moment, but Karen shows us that we will find it if we analyze events and circumstances to seek His hand.

Keep on asking, and you will receive what you ask for. Keep on seeking, and you will find. Keep on knocking, and the door will be opened to you. Matthew 7:7 NLT

I hope and pray that this book will inspire you to seek God for the significance of your own story and share it with others. Just as Karen shares her story, giving all the glory to God, you can do the same.

After reading *Back to Hope*, I was inspired to ask God to show me how He worked in the pivotal moments of my life. He continues to reveal why I went through those circumstances to be right here, right now, living for His plan, not mine.

Now it's your turn. Read and search your heart, anticipating that your Heavenly Father will reveal His hand in your life–past, present, and future.

I'm wildly cheering you on!

Alita Reynolds

President | Women of Faith

A Letter to the Reader

When faced with hardship, we get only one chance to steward the moment. We can trust, hope, praise, and worship in it, or we can turn from the Lord and strive to find our own understanding and make our own way. As you will read in my story, I have gone down both paths throughout my life, but now, matured in my faith, I choose to steward with trust and hope. After all, Jesus endured the cross because there was HOPE on the other side of it. You will never be overtaken by a situation if you have HOPE—not the popular societal hope we allude to when we casually say "I hope this happens." No, biblical hope is surrendering. Just as Jesus demonstrated, it's a laying down of one's life, pain, desires, dreams, and disappointments at the feet of the Lord because you have a joyful expectation of what He will do with it. To have hope means to die to oneself and to want only His will for your life, believing that it is good and the desires of your heart will be fulfilled.

I am a redheaded second child of four with stories of trauma, spiritual battles, and miraculous healing. I've faced anxiety, an eating disorder, Lyme disease, and many unexpected challenges life has a way of throwing at us. My story is chock full of hardship, but it is also full of surrender and desperation for the Lord, which allowed Him to remind me of His faithfulness and, ultimately, point me back to joy and hope. I believe we can find clues about our purpose by exploring what God has allowed us to walk through and what we feel passionate about in the way of ministering to and encouraging others. I have discovered my passion and purpose—to set captives free.

Setting captives free, to me, means pointing others back to their identity and worth in the Lord, back to God's faithfulness, and back to hope through their own personal encounters with the Holy Spirit so they can move forward in the joy and peace that Jesus died for them to have. I have found that one of the most powerful ways to do this is by exploring our stories. It starts with plotting and organizing our life stories to make sense of the memories. We look for different seasons and transformations within us that occurred between them. Then, we examine our memories to identify where God was clearly leading and speaking to us. Next, we pursue the Holy Spirit as we enter the places in our stories that still hold pain, requiring forgiveness and healing. Finally, we imagine the next chapter and take an active role in writing it by identifying the desires of our hearts and what living a life as our true, authentic selves, the way God created us, would look like. Ultimately, the narrative process leads to finding meaning, gaining healing, understanding one's identity, and engaging in the creation of a life of joy and purpose.

I have done this process myself and am excited to invite you into my story. I pray that as you witness what God has done in my life, you will find hooks of hope to hold fast to as you collect your own to offer others.

I am not an amazing woman, but what God has done in my life through the surrender is nothing less than absolutely amazing. None of us are perfect, and we are all on our own journeys. I share accounts of my experiences from a place of authenticity and vulnerability. Those in my story have their own versions and realities of the same events, and I value their stories, too.

"But how can people call for help if they don't know who to trust? And how can they know who to trust if they haven't heard of the One who can be trusted? And how can they hear if nobody tells them? And how is anyone going to tell them, unless someone is sent to do it?"
- Romans 10:14-15

I am here to tell you about the One you can trust. Welcome to my story, my testimony of God's faithfulness. I am so glad you are here.

CHAPTER ONE

The Early Years That Shaped Me

I was born "sunny side up," per my mom—face to the sky with jaundice, peach fuzzy hair on top of my head, and a swollen right eye because I was missing a tear duct. She says a few weeks later, the doctors bound my body to keep me from moving and drilled a tear duct without anesthesia. Back then, in the late seventies, they didn't believe babies felt pain. It's crazy that we are only forty-five years away from that ignorance. My mom says she walked to the parking lot to escape my screams, yet she still heard them.

I have no memory of this, but I know my body does. Thoughts and emotions are matter after all; they are chemical messengers stored in our bodies. So, whether we remember the events or not, we carry the emotional memories. Dr. Caroline Leaf's book, *Switch On Your Brain*, shares a neuroscience study that found over eighty-seven percent of physical ailments are emotionally based and operate at an unconscious level. Similarly, in Dr. Bruce Lipton's book, *The Biology of Belief: Unleashing the Power of Consciousness, Matter, and Miracles*, he shares that at least ninety-five percent of our cognitive activity is driven out of our unconscious mind. The good news is that the brain is neuroplastic, so as we heal emotionally and our beliefs change, the lens through which we see life and operate out of also changes. Incredible, right?

Some of the earliest conscious memories I hold consist of me sitting on a couch in our living room, probably about two to three years old, watching *Winnie the Pooh*. I was an early riser, so my brother, eighteen months my senior, was typically still sleeping. My dad could usually be found working in the yard; he was incredible at landscaping. My mom was usually doing chores or tinkering around in the kitchen. For the most part, I was a peaceful child and was good at entertaining myself, but loved to play with my brother and our neighborhood friends when given the chance.

We lived in Fort Lauderdale, Florida, and had a pool in our backyard. My dad built a beautiful deck around it with a friend named Norm, who needed better-fitting shorts because he had what we refer to as a "plumber's butt." At three years old, I used to say, "Ew, Norm, I can see your butt," while he sweated and labored over our deck. At first, it was a legitimate response to what I was seeing, but I soon learned that my dad loved when I said it. To hear my dad laugh and know I was responsible for it was a great feeling. From an early age, like all children, I craved the attention of my father, but didn't always like the way I received it. For instance, one day, scared to swim on my own, my dad got frustrated and threw me into the deep end of the pool. I'm sure he didn't mean it maliciously, but I was not happy about his approach, even though it was successful. I learned quickly and have been swimming ever since.

At around age four, I attended a summer camp where they would check our heads for lice weekly. They told me that redheads were more likely to get it. Well, I never did, and I don't think there's any truth to that anyway. As if the pale skin and dark brown freckles that accompanied my flaming red hair weren't enough for me to wish I had been made differently. I so wanted to have golden tan skin. However, there was a leader at the camp who would tell us how uniquely made we all were and that there were no duplicate people in the world—even twins had differences.

Thinking about God choosing my hair, eye, and skin color somehow took the sting out of the longing I had to look different. I listened to a podcast the other day in which the host said that God imagined and created each of us. Something about that hit me hard: He imagined each of us, thought of us, and created each of us for a unique purpose in His mind before He physically created us. He has a purpose for everything He does and for all of His creation. I just loved the fresh way this revelation resonated with my spirit.

From as early as I can remember, I spent at least half my time at my friend Janel's house next door. We rode big wheels, played in our pool, and acted out dramatic scenes from the soap operas our mothers watched during the day. I remember that her grandmother, who lived with them, used bar soap to brush her teeth. I thought that was pretty strange, but I didn't care, her family was very nice, and I always felt welcome in their home.

Janel and I also went to the same church. I would go to Catholic Mass and attend Confraternity of Christian Doctrine (CCD) classes each week. In one class, I choked on a piece of candy. My mom was teaching, and I didn't want to interrupt her, so I ran into the kitchen and flagged down a woman who frantically tried to help me. I got it out on my own, but I remember thinking at that moment, *Wow, I might die.* As heavy as my conversation with the Lord was as I begged Him to help me, once the candy came up, I carried on as if I never had that life-threatening experience. I honestly don't know if I ever even told my mom. It's interesting how quickly we move past powerful moments of God's hand moving in our lives.

Janel and I also attended the same dance school. I took dance classes from the age of two to about eight years old. I was in advanced classes and received positive affirmations that were crucial to the development of how I understood others to see me. Like any child, I wanted to stand out and be told that I was good at something. Children need to be assured that they have value; dance provided that for me. I loved dance recitals, being on stage, and the rush I would get. I was one of the girls that the other girls watched to remember the steps as their nerves kicked in and they forgot. I was proud and happy to do that; I was a natural-born leader and felt responsible for the success of all the dancers on the stage with me.

Some very special memories I carry from dance recitals are wearing one of my dad's big button-down shirts over my costume on the way to the recital and knowing my entire family would be in the audience to cheer me on. My mom even had a costume that matched mine made for my Cabbage Patch doll one year. I loved the days after recitals almost as much as recital days because I was still riding high on the joy of it all. I also still had leftover makeup on, and for that day, my pale eyelashes and eyebrows had definition, and I thought I looked pretty.

When I was six, we moved, and I started a new school, I think because of the proximity to our home. I don't remember it being a difficult transition, and I made friends quickly. In the summer between first and second grades, I did some sort of intelligence or placement test at my school. The one question I didn't get credit for was "What are the four seasons?" I forgot about fall because we didn't really get one in Florida. I guess I did well enough because I was placed in a gifted and talented class for the second and third grades. I knew this meant they thought I was smart, and much like the accolades I received for my dancing, it gave me a confidence boost that would continue to carry me throughout my schooling.

I don't have many memories of making trouble as a child, but I was never afraid to stand up for myself, which often meant talking back. I knew my parents meant business when they were mad. The words "Wait until your father gets home" were said to my siblings and me pretty often by our mom. This meant a spanking would be had when he did get home. I also remember my mom cleaning my mouth out with a bar of soap when I talked back and how it tasted when the chunks got stuck in my teeth (another reason I thought it strange that Janel's grandmother brushed her teeth with bar soap—I knew how bad it tasted).

We lived near my mom's parents and would often swim in their pool while my mom, aunts, and grandmother played backgammon. I longed to be one of the grown-up women who got to stay indoors and talk over snacks and coffee. My grandparents smoked cigarettes in their home, so I would come home with bloodshot, burning eyes from the chlorine in the pool and smoke in the air, and toes raw from climbing their pool's edge to get in and out. I was always sunburnt and had water in my ears. I used to have to drink the pink medicine (Amoxicillin) often because I had frequent ear infections. I got tubes in my ears toward the end of first grade and never had issues with ear infections again.

My brother played baseball, and I loved going to his games because I had a major crush on his friend Jason, who was on his team. I had the iconic eighties feathered hair and would go into the bathroom to flip my head back and forth to fluff it up before I said hi to Jason when he came over. I would also blast Whitney Houston's song, "How Will I Know," over and over from my boombox as I jumped on my mini trampoline in the backyard while Jason and my brother fished in the canal. This was my first memory of really wanting to be noticed by a boy.

I played soccer with my brother on a co-ed team, but I cared more about the flowers and dancing in the grass than what was happening on the field. It drove my dad, and especially my brother, who was embarrassed, crazy. The cherry on top was when I looked up to see the ball coming to me one game and, with vigor and determination, dribbled it all the way to the net to make what would be the only goal in my soccer career. Unfortunately, as it turned out, I was dribbling to the wrong goal and scored a point for the other team. That was the last year I played on my brother's team. I wasn't a very competitive child; I am still not competitive with other people, but I'm always yearning to somehow better myself.

Florida had the coolest sun showers, where it would rain in your backyard and not your front yard, or vice versa. The sun showers would happen often but thunderstorms were my favorite. I still love the rain. I have a sign in my home office that reads, "I like people who smile when it's raining." I appreciate its metaphorical application of being drawn to people who can smile when circumstances may not be ideal; they can rise above. But I also truly love the rain and jibe with others who share my affinity.

I have learned that people who love rain tend to be "negative ion" people. We negative ion people don't love bright sunshine and feel the best in overcast weather. I like to say it's my Irish roots. My older brother made fun of me for liking thunderstorms, saying that I just liked them because it meant we all had to stay inside together. He wasn't wrong. These were the days of leaving the house at sunrise and not coming home until sundown. I remember almost feeling unwelcome at home, like I was doing something wrong if I wasn't outside playing.

I am an extroverted introvert. I love people and am outgoing, but I also need my downtime to process my thoughts and emotions. I think as a child I felt exhausted and overwhelmed often because I rarely got time to rest and feel the comfort of those I loved curled up on the couch. So, when God provided those opportunities, it was refreshing to my soul, and I didn't care if my brother made fun of me for it.

In the eighties (for all of my younger readers), we waited for toy catalogs to come in the mail and for the commercials during Saturday morning cartoons, as they inspired our lists of gifts we hoped to receive for birthdays and Christmas. Some of my favorite things were the plastic charm necklaces and bracelets. I loved collecting charms (the little plastic bottle with fake milk in it was my favorite). I also had a redheaded My Child doll named "Eric," and I took him everywhere.

My brother collected baseball cards, and I had a sticker collection. We would get pizza next to a baseball card shop that also sold stickers, and it was always a fun night when we got to go there, and even more fun when we were home and got to add to our collections. One of my prized possessions was my very own typewriter, which my grandmother gifted me. I would approach typing with nervous excitement because I loved to write, but every time I did, I would skin my fingers at the cuticles as they slipped under the keys. It did not thwart my writing, however. I had an incredible imagination and wrote short stories that won school awards in second grade.

We didn't take many vacations when I was younger, but we would visit my dad's parents about four hours away in Daytona. I would get car sick every time and would often spend the entire first day recovering in bed. We had cousins, all older than me, who lived near my grandparents. We always had fun together, playing hide and seek (never in my grandfather's shop, mind you), and one of my cousins would braid my hair. I loved it because the next day when I took the braid out, my stick-straight hair had waves in it. I also got her hand-me-down clothes and was so grateful because I pretty much thought she was the coolest. Even though they did not live close, throughout my life, it comforted me to know I had family out there who loved me.

We would spend most holidays with my mom's family. Christmas Eve was always our biggest family gathering and celebration of the year. My mom didn't have a lot when she was growing up, so she would go above and beyond for holidays and celebrations in our home. I don't know where she learned how to do it, but I remember our living room looking like a scene right out of a movie on Christmas mornings: lights on the tree, glittery wrapping paper, and piles upon piles of gifts. Thanksgiving was also always full of good food and time together. Creating magical and memorable holidays for my family is something I learned from her.

I had a younger sister three years my junior and a surprise little brother eight years my junior (although I am pretty sure we were all surprises in some way) who were born during these years. My baby brother was born by emergency cesarean section, and my mom got a horrible infection afterward because the surgeons left a sponge inside her abdomen. She had to be hospitalized to receive antibiotics. When we went to visit her at the hospital, she asked me how it was going with us home with our dad. I answered in a whisper but loud enough for him to hear, "Fine, but he doesn't do laundry." It made both my mom and dad laugh. He knew it was true, and I knew he was doing as well as he could while worrying about his wife and caring for four children on his own.

My little brother was born with one long, gray hair that stuck out of his forehead. We used to say it was because his birth was so traumatic that it gave him gray hair. The umbilical cord was wrapped around his neck and had knots in it. The fact that he survived was a miracle. I loved every minute I was allowed to help take care of him; it was like he was my real-life baby doll. He was always a funny baby and toddler, and he was a welcome addition to our clan.

My sister and I are very close now, but the younger years were a bit more difficult. I remember my mom pressuring me to play with her when what I really wanted to do was things that were a bit more for older kids, like follow my brother and his friends into very dark and scary drain pipes in our neighborhood and play soccer in the cul-de-sac. My sister and I did have some neighborhood friends we would play with, and we liked to play with our dolls together. We also got into trouble together sometimes, and I'm pretty sure it was always my fault. I remember one day we soaped up our bare butts during a bath and proceeded to put our butt prints on the wall, which apparently were hard to get off. This may have been one of the earned spankings.

Something I did often as a child was lie in bed and talk to the Lord. I would try to imagine if there was no God, no world, no universe; if there was nothing at all. My brain would eventually feel like it was short-circuiting; no human brain can comprehend such things. Have you ever done that?

I remember God speaking to me for the first time one evening, when I was about seven, as I lay on my bed. He whispered, "You will do great things." From that point on, I always felt like He was with me. I had a desire to make Him proud, and I was hopeful and excited about the "great things" He had planned. People sometimes ask me how I know I heard the Lord or what He actually sounds like. It is usually my own voice in my head, but it's always random, not something I am thinking about. It also always comes with a "knowing" of sorts in my spirit that it was the Lord—kind of like an energy shift or a warm breeze in your soul. It also always seems to answer something I've been praying about, or encourages in a way I need.

It always brings peace and aligns with or illuminates the Word of God. I wish I could explain it better than that. More than anything, I pray you have your own powerful encounters with the Lord and that He will soften your heart to hear

His voice. I know there are people who don't believe God is alive, active, speaking to His people, or performing miracles. To that, all I can say is that my God, the One True Living God, *is*, and He is available to all of us.

As you can see, I have many fun memories of being a child. But I was also a deep feeler and an even deeper thinker. I was an observer of people. I remember randomly crying a lot. My mom would ask why I was crying, and I would either truly not know or would be too afraid to tell her, but my response was always, "I don't know." And now, I still don't have all the details, but I have a better understanding. I have discovered recently that painful things happened to me as a child that I've blocked out. Even subconsciously, this has affected my identity, confidence, every relationship, and every decision I have made throughout my life. The lens through which I experienced life was broken.

We all experience hard things during childhood—traumas of varying degrees. As children, we learn how to interact with and perceive the world, and our world often includes adults who are still hurt and broken and who haven't done their own healing work. As the saying goes, "Hurt people hurt people." I don't want to be someone who hurts others because I haven't done my own work. For me, doing the work means breaking down the negative beliefs and agreements I have made with the enemy in my life because of my trauma, and pursuing the Lord, His truth, and my identity in Him more and more.

I have learned that in order for us to find freedom from what others have given to us because of their own brokenness, we need to surrender to the Lord for His understanding and healing. We need to forgive those who have hurt us and also ask the Lord for forgiveness for any negative beliefs or coping mechanisms we operate in due to harm done to us. James 5:16 points out that we will be healed by confessing our sins and praying for others. This is a way back to hope for the future and the purpose that He has for each of us.

CHAPTER TWO
A Move and a Family Fractured

In the middle of my third-grade year, we moved to Arkansas for my dad's job. I remember a friend of the family asking if they wore shoes in Arkansas and if there were any McDonald's restaurants. That, understandably, made me apprehensive about what I was in for, but the move would be an adventure. I loved adventures, so I was hesitantly optimistic and hopeful, and I had no choice; we were moving whether I liked it or not.

I went from a gifted and talented classroom in Florida to a third-grade classroom in an Arkansas public school that, I would venture to guess, didn't have great funding or resources. It was frustrating because the only academic challenges I encountered were spelling tests because I couldn't understand my teacher's thick southern accent. There was a group of girls threatening daily to beat me up because they said the boys "liked" me; this caused daily anxiety about going to school. None of this was an issue in Florida. We never talked about "liking" or "going with" anyone. I got a note passed to me on day one of the new school from a boy. *Will you go with me?* I responded, *Go where?* and the classroom erupted in laughter. Apparently, having boyfriends and girlfriends in third grade was just commonplace in this Arkansas school, and they called it "going with" one another. I crumpled up his note and threw it away, and for the rest of the year, I begged him to leave me alone. He embarrassed me, and I did not crave his or anyone else's attention. I just wanted to blend in.

I made some friends at school and started taking gymnastics. I wish I had stuck with dance; I was good at it, and it was part of me. It helped me express my emotions and challenged me physically and mentally. Unfortunately, I took classes at one school and did not like it. Everything and everyone were so different. I was discouraged and did not want to even try other dance schools. Grieving dance, my teacher, and friends, I found gymnastics to be just *okay*. However, I liked my coach and my friends. As I continued on with lessons, I gained more skills and confidence and enjoyed it more.

I could do all kinds of cool tumbling tricks. To this day, when I hear Rob Base & DJ EZ Rock's "It Takes Two," I am transported back to those days of stepping up for my turn to tumble down the mat, filled with nervous excitement. I would be so anxious about upcoming gymnastics competitions that when show air dates were advertised on TV, I would think, *I will be so happy on that day*—but not because of the show. I knew I'd be relieved because it would be the day after the gymnastics meet, and it would be over. I never shied away from the challenge, though. I pressed into the nerves and allowed myself to grow in the discomfort of it all. When I got to the point in my training that I was moving into higher levels and was learning to do flips on the balance beam, however, I decided I wasn't passionate about it enough to risk breaking my neck, so I quit.

When we moved, my family and I started attending a Catholic church called Immaculate Conception (IC), and outside of church, I continued to spend time with the Lord in the way I did, and still do, by praying and journaling. I was becoming bolder in my faith. One night, I went to a sleepover with some of my new friends from school and gymnastics. We must have been watching either VH1 or MTV because a heavy metal band came on. I do not remember which one; all I remember is the evil I felt. I was immediately propelled up from my sleeping bag on the floor. I turned off the TV and started praying out loud that all evil would leave the room and the house. The girls looked at me with wide eyes, and I barely knew what had just happened. I never really prayed out loud except with my family before meals with the simple "Bless us, oh Lord, for these Thy gifts" type of thing. God was growing my discernment and confidence in Him. Thank goodness my friends were kind and did not make fun of me or make me feel bad about the random, and probably awkwardly done, spiritual warfare.

My siblings and I had neighborhood friends who we spent most of our time with. Arkansas experienced a record snowstorm our first year there, and it was the first time we had ever seen snow. We had no snow or cold weather gear, so we put plastic bags over our cotton gloves, multiple layers of sweatpants and sweatshirts on, and ventured out for as long as we could stand it, come back in, defrost, and repeat. We built an igloo with our friends, and it was epic. That summer, we adventured around our neighborhood in new, scary, and dark drain pipes, as well as swam in a dirty old creek not far from our house. I don't even want to know what else was swimming in that creek.

In fourth grade, my siblings and I were able to move off of the waitlist into a small Catholic school that was affiliated with our church. I absolutely loved it. I loved religion class, that we went to Mass each week as a school, and just the overall atmosphere and culture. I also felt challenged academically again. After gymnastics, I returned to soccer. I was the only girl on IC's co-ed soccer team, and my coach would tell the boys that if they played as defensively as I did, we would win all the games. I won't lie, it felt good to be noticed, and I loved to make my coach proud. I also felt powerful when I was on the field.

Sadly, one player on my team, David, found out he had a malignant brain tumor. I witnessed him walk out his journey in a way that strengthened my faith. He was wrapped in tremendous peace. He would speak in our gym in front of the entire school, comforting us. Can you imagine? I think he was a year above me, so he would've been in fifth grade. He ended up passing away, and at his funeral, I sat with my eyes fixed on his mom. I was witnessing pure grief. It was hard to watch, but it showed me the reality of the pain that life could bring and how to surrender to it. After all, we have to feel in order to heal, a lesson I am still learning today. David's passing, in addition to my mom needing an emergency hysterectomy, left me with anxiety that would keep me from being able to sleep most of my fourth-grade year. I would get anxious as the sun set because I knew I would lie awake in bed fighting thoughts of what life would be like if my mom died and feeling vulnerable about my own mortality.

I did not keep in touch with my friends from the public

school, but I made new ones. One friend, Leigha, and I became close almost immediately. She walked up to me at lunch. I think it was one of the good lunches, you know, with the instant mashed potatoes, gravy, and fried chicken.

"Are you mad at me?" she asked. I was; she had hurt my feelings somehow at recess.

"Yes," I replied candidly, "I am mad at you." She was shocked and said no one was ever honest with her like that; we were instantly best friends. Complete opposites, Leigha was tall with dark curly hair, the bronze skin I dreamed of having, long lanky limbs on her tall frame, and an extrovert. I was of average height, pale, bright red hair, an athletic build, and, as you know, was an introvert. We balanced each other out.

We loved cheetos (not the Cheetos brand cheetos but the generic brands) because they were cheesier and crunchier. We would put napkins on the middle of the lunch table and dump our generic cheetos and Ruffles together in a pile to share. Every once in a while, a nice boy would give me his bag of cheetos. He sat behind me in class. I have memories of playing with small white daisies that were patched on my over-the-chair fabric cubby made by my mom as I turned around in my seat to talk with him. I'm pretty sure this nice boy, who would bring me cheetos occasionally and sit behind me, had a crush on me. Well, I know he did because his mom told my mom he asked if it was "okay to like a redhead." (Insert head scratch, right?)

It makes me laugh now. We blue-eyed redheads are less than one percent of the world's population, so I am sure I was an enigma to him. I mean, he was smart and well-read. He probably read tales of redheads being hanged or burned at the stake as witches just because of the color of their hair.

I also remember a woman at the grocery store one day saying she wished her son could meet me because he liked redheads, and she followed it by saying, "People either love or hate redheads." It's interesting when you explore messages you got as a child and how they may have affected you, such as "You may be evil," "You're weird and different," and "People either love or hate you based on how you look."

IC was a kindergarten through eighth grade school, so I was able to remain with a consistent cohort of friends and classmates through eighth grade. In fifth grade, I gave up soccer so I could join the basketball team with my friends. It was challenging in the best way. We had an amazing coach who loved to win, and win we did. Leigha and I became obsessed with the New Kids on the Block, and you could hear their songs flooding from my room wallpapered in Donnie Wahlberg posters most days.

We were a busy family with four kids, four cats, and a dog. All of us kids were involved in extracurricular activities. When we moved, my dad actually started traveling, which was ironic. *Why have us move just to send him to another state to work?* He was gone all week, and when he was home on the weekends, he would golf. I missed his presence. I didn't have a deeply emotional relationship with my dad, but I knew my mom was happier with him around. He brought a certain lightness and fun to the house when he was in a good mood. However, the laugh I learned to love as a child was not heard as often during this time. Something shifted in him and in their marriage after the move. Probably many things.

Whether it was true or not, from my perspective as a child, I always felt like a nuisance to my dad, like he was thinking, *I wish these kids weren't here,* or maybe, *I wish I wasn't here.* So, if that were the case, his traveling could've potentially been a good thing because there would've been less tension in the home as he was somewhere else, maybe even where he preferred to be. However, it was not a good thing for my mom. She was an overwhelmed stay-at-home mom, and now, being a wife myself, I am sure she felt lonely, abandoned, and probably quite angry. She became emotionally unavailable, dealing with her own disappointment. Her father also died shortly after we moved to Arkansas, and she'd just left her entire family, whom we were very close to. She had made no true friends, and I am sure she felt weary; now not only left to fend for herself but her four children as well, on her own. The adventurous move that had many positive outcomes also resulted in what felt like a fracture in our family, and I did not feel secure.

I'm an adult now and know how complicated life and relationships can be. I have learned to give grace and forgive when painful memories come up for me. And being a parent of a teenager and a young adult myself, I am now faced with the pain my husband and I have caused in their lives. The truth is, most of us don't come into adulthood without scars, with it all figured out. It's quite the opposite. The child-rearing years are the hardest because they also seem to overlap with finding our footing in adulthood, marriage, and financial stress as we forge our career paths and all the pressure that brings.

If you read through my journals from when my kids were young, my consistent prayer was that God would protect them from our junk and that I would parent and live in such a way that I would have no regrets. I was mindful of how I parented; I thought I was present and available, but I made mistakes. I was distracted and often emotionally detached because of the methods I learned to cope in my own childhood, as well as the challenges I was experiencing in my marriage, school, and career responsibilities.

What I do now is pray that the Lord will stir the areas in my children that need healing so they can be healed and set free. The hardest thing in the world is to watch your child share the pain and heartbreak they felt as children because of you. But I am here for it. I hold space, and they are safe to share. I feel blessed that they are willing to share. I sit with them in their pain, listen, apologize, and love them through it. Then, I get in the lap of the Lord with all of the sadness I feel for them, repent, and thank Him that He fills all of the gaps and heals the wounds that I was either part of or couldn't protect them from.

The truth is, even in our best efforts, we cannot be everything someone else needs. Only the Lord can be that, so we need to pray that our children earnestly seek the Lord, thirst for Him, and long for Him with their whole being (Psalm 63:1). When they encounter Him, He will grow their confidence and heal their wounds. One thing I know for sure is that my mom did this. I inherited her book, *The Power of a Praying Parent* by Stormie Omartian, and it was well-worn. I am positive that her prayers were more powerful than any weapons formed against us.

CHAPTER THREE
Adolescence and the Pressure to be Perfect

Transitioning into junior high school and adolescence, I felt anxious and rarely experienced peace in our home. My mom struggled more and more, and that meant there was yelling, anger, and a powerful spirit of unrest and anxiety. My nervous system was always on high alert, and I was chronically in a state of fight or flight. If I didn't feel like a nuisance and burden before, I did then. At the time, of course, I knew nothing of spiritual warfare. If I had, I would've prayed through my home and for my family. I just knew how I felt, and I was drowning, along with my mom.

I became close with another girl in our school whose parents were having problems at home (marriage is hard). She struggled with depression and became hyper-focused on her appearance. She did not like how she looked (being a teenager is also hard). She listened to R.E.M. and other bands from the time that were considered alternative rock. These bands often produced depressing and dark music. Listening to "Everybody Hurts" on repeat was not great for conjuring joy. These were also the days when MTV's *Real Life, Spring Break,* and other shows on TV overly glorified "sexy" and "thin" women. I think women have always been sexualized because, well, God made us beautiful, but there was something different about this time period. There was a strong movement of overtly and disrespectfully objectifying women and placing an incredible amount of value and worth on how we looked—in particular, how skinny we were.

The enemy who rules the airways was taking advantage of having more access to us through television shows and larger technological advances. Teen-targeted magazines only made matters worse with airbrushed and edited versions of real girls and women who were made to look like surreal, flawless, unattainable fantasies for the men whose affection and attention we were somehow supposed to attract and whose love we were supposed to earn. It felt like we had failed in society's eyes, in the eyes of our male counterparts, and most certainly in our own eyes, by just being ourselves and developing naturally into young women.

The teen years were a difficult transition period as it was. I didn't know who I was, where I fit in, who I was going to become, or what my future would hold. I had to navigate these questions while my body was growing and changing in ways I couldn't control, and I was being judged by how I looked. Scared to death of what the end product would be, with every new development, I compared and tediously picked myself apart. I never felt like I was good enough.

Like the perfect storm, it was also at this time that Weight Watchers was popular, advertisements about diet programs were in every commercial break, and dieting was often the topic of conversation on *Oprah*, which I watched faithfully every day. I remember thinking that just being an adult in America meant I would have to strive my whole life not to be obese and unhealthy. I would have to restrict my diet and go to great lengths to not become what society was clearly representing as a failure in some way. In my eighth-grade mind, I refused to become a disappointment. I would prove that I had self-control.

I have always been a researcher by nature, so in my determination to be healthy and to be "enough," I studied weight loss. As a result, I understood that monitoring calories in versus calories out was the way to ensure I did not become obese. This, plus all the diet commercials, resulted in my diet becoming pretty much anything that boasted "fat-free" and "sugar-free," which, ironically, were the most inflammatory and unhealthy foods. I now know that the poor quality of our food is largely why there is a weight problem on a national scale. Many people get an excess of calories but are nutrient-starved, which leads to many health issues, including obesity.

Also, at this time, I was drawn to Susan Powter, who would come on my television at night. She taught emphatically about eating only fat-free food and, if I recall correctly, that we should all be eating potatoes. Whatever she was preaching, I was buying it. She was enthusiastic, seemed confident in what she was screaming as she ran across the stage, and had the body type I wanted: toned and strong. Convinced I could do it and that I could hold tight to this movement, I made up my mind. I would control what I ate and, thus, control how my body developed; I would be enough.

Leigha and I drifted apart because she wanted to have fun and be a kid, but I was dealing with depression and what felt like a broken family. At this time in my life, I could relate more to my friend who was also depressed and had trouble at home. We grew closer, and one day she decided she and I were the "fat ones" out of our group of friends. That's literally what she presented to me: "We are the fat ones." I was not overweight, and neither was she. I had a very athletic and healthy build, but I was not long and lanky like Leigha and another girl, Katey, in our friend group, so maybe I wasn't good enough.

Her declaration felt like a call to action. With my recent decision to control how my body developed, it felt like a good time to enact a plan, and I figured it might be easier with a partner. She introduced me to ipecac syrup, a medication that is used to induce vomiting in the event someone ingests something toxic (to this day, I cannot smell or ingest syrup without feeling nauseous). Each time I took a dose, I would call someone to talk to who could distract me as the fear welled, knowing what was coming. The crippling nausea was followed by violent episodes of vomiting. I never binged; I would just take the syrup after any normal meal when I felt the uncomfortable feeling of being full and felt that I had failed.

I hated vomiting, and I hated the feeling of nausea. Plus, I really wasn't eating much because I wasn't hungry due to the stress in my body. I decided it would be easier to just not eat. I was able to distract attention from myself by "doing everything right." I made good grades and stayed busy, so with three other kids, my parents didn't notice I was restricting. If someone mentioned my not eating, I would just give an excuse like I had already eaten or didn't feel well. The confusing thing was that people were complimenting me on how I looked. I knew the only thing that was different was that I was restricting how much I ate, and, though I hadn't lost much, I was losing weight.

During spring break of our eighth-grade year, the friend who introduced me to ipecac syrup invited me to go to the beach with her and her family. I was beginning to look thin but not yet unwell. I think her parents may have thought *I* was the one who introduced disordered eating behaviors to their daughter, instead of the other way around. I don't know what conversations were happening behind my back. They looked at me with judgment in their eyes, and shame started to build.

My friend met a boy on that trip, and during the summer between our eighth and ninth-grade years, she snuck out of her home in the middle of the night to hitchhike from Arkansas to wherever he lived. I found out she ran away when her mother called mine, angry, assuming I had known and that I had something to do with it. She and her husband wanted their daughter to have nothing to do with me. It must have been an extremely scary time for them, and it was probably easier to blame me than to see their own brokenness and how it had affected my friend.

Shortly after this, I learned that she had a drug problem and had been sexually promiscuous as well. She had been sneaking out for months, all while I was asleep, oblivious, in her bed having what I thought was just a normal sleepover with a friend. We would wake up together and continue on without a mention on her end or a suspicion on mine. Once her parents retrieved her from this boy's home, she went to rehab, and I spiraled as I tried not to break into a million tiny pieces. I had no idea about her secret life, and it crushed me. This was my first experience with betrayal and deception by someone close to me that I trusted. In one day, I lost all sense of confidence in myself. *How had I missed it?* I lost my best friend, the one I would usually call to talk about my pain, but she was also the reason I was hurting. I was reeling. The only control or sense of security I had left was in the rituals of food restriction.

I started my ninth-grade year at an all-girls' private Catholic school called Mount Saint Mary ("the Mount" for short). It was a dream for someone like me in the season I was in. It was a challenging college preparatory school, and I was enrolled in all Advanced Placement (AP) classes. I had plenty of schoolwork to fill my mind, time, and space, which served as my excuse for why I wouldn't be able to join my family for meals. My dad was still gone in every sense of the word; my mom was still unhappy, and our home felt anything but peaceful and joyful.

I hold few memories of my siblings during this time of my life. I went so deep within myself, or maybe so far outside of myself, that all I remember is studying and wishing I was invisible. Leigha and Katey became my lifelines during this time. The three of us would have lunch together every day, and they never said anything to me about the fact that I would study instead of eat. They never said anything about the fact that I had lost twenty pounds off an already small frame in only about three months' time. They would just let me be with them and feel safe.

I remember watching my friends and the other girls in school; they were happy, bouncy (they seemed to skip and bounce instead of walk), and hyper—or maybe they just had joy. I would wonder what was wrong with me as I picked at iceberg lettuce and fat-free French dressing, adding up the calories in my head. Leigha and Katey had crushes on boys, and seemingly no stress or care in the world other than making plans for the weekend. I couldn't imagine ever wanting a boy to notice me, or that one ever would for that matter. I also feared the level of vulnerability that I knew a relationship would require. But deep down, I wanted the normal teen experience; it looked like pure freedom but it didn't feel like it was for me. Watching my friends and the other girls and the light they danced in gave me hope for what life could be. It also highlighted my own hopelessness because I felt broken and didn't know how to fix myself. I didn't know how to break through the darkness to get there.

    I joined the cross country team because, well, I wanted to burn even more calories; I wanted to push myself to the limit. I wanted to hurt physically so it would overpower the pain I felt emotionally. I no longer had control; the eating disorder did. My coach was Mrs. Arndt, and she was maybe the only person in my life who truly saw me. She was brave enough to cross the line between not being a parent and being someone who cared and couldn't act like nothing was happening. She kept me after class to ask me if I was eating and told me she knew I was lying when I said I was. Coach Arndt met the addiction head-on and didn't back down; instead, she tried to do what she could to help set me free. She set up meetings with a few of the other teachers who were vegetarians because I had also become a vegetarian as an excuse for why I was so thin. She wanted them to teach me how to be a healthy vegetarian. It was a hard sell because these women were overweight; they were everything I didn't want to be, except they did seem happy and confident. I wondered what that must feel like—to just be comfortable in your own skin. To feel you are enough just as you are. I appreciated them, and what Coach Arndt was trying to do, but it didn't work.

    Coach Arndt was putting pressure on me to make a change, or I would not be able to stay on the team. If only it could have been that easy. We ran early in the mornings before school. I remember freezing and being so tired most mornings that I would try to sleep and run hills at the same time. I could never master it. After our runs, we would shower before school started, and I remember how good it felt being clean from the inside out. Running allowed me to burn off the cortisol that seemed to always course through my anxious body. It was a release. However, mid-sophomore year, I quit cross country because it was becoming too difficult in my struggle. I was tired, and I was tired of having to eat to maintain energy for running and for Coach Arndt to let me stay on the team. I knew I was disappointing her, and I knew her concern came from a place of love, which made me feel even worse.

What was surprising and terrifying to me at the time was that when I stopped running, my weight dropped dramatically. I would wake up with bruises on the inside of my knees because when I slept on my side, there was no fat, no padding, and my body was nutrient-starved. I was freezing all of the time. At school I would count down the hours until I could get home to soak in a hot bathtub or burrow under a heating blanket. I was starting to burn muscle. I was no longer restricting to lose weight; I had just lost all sensitivity to feeling hungry. I knew I was too thin, and the number on the scale dropped daily.

"Karen, you have lost so much weight," the girls at school who cared about me would say. And in my defense, I would retort, "That's because I don't eat." I wasn't hiding it; I couldn't. I felt the judgmental and concerned stares from classmates and teachers.

"I know," I wanted to scream. "And I don't know what to do! I can't break free. It owns me now. Just look away!"

What makes me the saddest about this time in my life is that I was so enveloped in myself, in my thoughts, in feelings of depression, in battling, that I was not able to be a friend, a sister, a daughter, a light, or an encouragement to anyone else. This is what the enemy likes to do: get us distracted, in any way that he can, so we are not usable to glorify the Lord and point others back to Him and His love.

During this time, I was bound by fear. I did not know how to get free and I did not know if I would live, but because I had friends and people around me who cared, I started to have faith that what I hoped for, freedom, could be a reality for me. Hebrews 11:1 says, "Now faith is confidence in what we hope for and assurance about what we do not see." I could not see how it was possible yet, but I was hoping for healing—for freedom.

CHAPTER FOUR

Nothing Left but a Surrender

Part of the curriculum at the Mount was personal spiritual work and Bible study. We would spend time in the chapel writing letters to our future selves, reflecting on where we were in our lives and where we wanted to be at the same time next year (a practice I still love and have taught my own children). Some teachers would lead us through guided meditations where we would encounter and sit with Jesus in our imaginations. They equipped us with practices for pressing into the Lord for a deeper relationship and spiritual growth. I know for some of the happy, bouncy girls this was a joke—just a fun break from classwork—but for me, it was the beginning of a series of encounters with the Holy Spirit that rescued me and allowed me to be alive and writing to you today.

Occasionally, when my dad was in town, he would slip research and news articles he had read about eating disorders under my door. In that small act, I felt he was showing me he cared; he loved me. He was showing me that he thought I was smart enough to see the written evidence and walk away from the choices I was making. Again, if only it were that easy. My mom, of course, noticed at this point and would wait to catch me running through the hall in my towel so she could confront me. She realized quickly that if she questioned me, she would slam into the walls of anger I had built around myself to hide. It was better to be angry and unapproachable because if no one wanted to be around me, no one would be, which meant no one could get close and I would remain safe in captivity.

Of course, my parents wanted me to eat and get over it; they needed me to be okay. Marriage and raising kids are hard enough; add something all-consuming like this to the mix, and it demands a pause. As adults, we aren't always good at taking a pause, right? It takes everyone being willing to hit the brakes and pay attention. It takes effort, time, love, vulnerability, and strength. As a parent, it requires you to engage in your own healing and owning where you contributed to the problem. It also takes a surrendering of our own plans.

I didn't want anyone to feel bad or sorry for me. I didn't want to be a nuisance or the focus of anyone's attention. I just wanted everyone to leave me alone. There was an internal tension I now wrestled with. I didn't want to give up the control and false sense of safety the addiction provided, but I also didn't want to die. I didn't want to be held captive, but I did not know where to even start on the journey to freedom. You're probably thinking, *Why didn't you just start eating?* Well, as I started doing my own research, I found that if I had been starving and then refed too fast, I could cause stress on my body. It wasn't prepared for the work of digestion. I would need to slowly reintroduce food.

I was scared to do it wrong because I also heard during

this time, whether accurate or not, that Karen Carpenter of the famous sibling duo The Carpenters, ironically enough also anorexic and my namesake, died from refeeding too quickly. I also read that my metabolism was most likely shut down from starvation, so anything I ingested would most likely be stored as fat, and I didn't want that either. I would need medical guidance and support.

One day in my tenth-grade year, the prayers of the many concerned onlookers and my mother were answered when my father was in town and did something more important than work. He entered the battle for his daughter. I got dressed in my plaid uniform skirt, a typical bun in my hair, and a comfy sweatshirt. My hundred-pound backpack was on, and I was ready to go, but I was informed that I wasn't going to school. My dad had spoken to someone at work about me, and they recommended an eating disorder clinic at the local children's hospital. We were going there instead.

I was scared and upset, but I felt relief I would never admit to—that I was finally getting help. I knew I would have to choose to join in the battle for my life. I had to tell the fighter in me to keep fighting, but that the focus needed to be on defeating the eating disorder and the control it had in my life by staying constantly submitted to the Lord in my heart and mind. I would need to keep my eyes on the new goal: freedom.

If my parents taking me to a treatment center had happened a little earlier on, before I had really started pressing into God and allowing Him to teach me to trust Him and find my security in Him, I may have kicked and screamed the whole way. But I was tired of fighting alone. I wanted to curl up in someone's lap and cry. I wanted to admit my weakness, give up control, and let others love and care for me. I had nothing left but a surrender. God's timing was perfect; He knew I was ready. So, piled in the big gray van, we rode in silence the whole way. My mom's nervous energy and my dad's determination filled the space; they were louder than any words that could be spoken. In my fifteen-year-old heart, I was having a conversation with God, which I had learned to do, and He was telling me to trust Him.

What a blessing it was to have such an amazing treatment facility nearby. I know many cities, or even states, don't. The elevator up to the eating disorder clinic was walled in mirrors. So, I stood staring at myself, facing how thin I had become. Once the paperwork was complete, they took us back to do the first thing: weigh. They did not share the number with me, but I knew. I checked multiple times a day, and I also knew the risks my body was facing being so thin and malnourished, namely, sudden cardiac arrest and seizures. I read all about it in the articles my dad shared.

We met with the medical doctor first, Dr. Portilla. She asked questions like, "What do you eat daily?" "What do you pack for school lunches?" and "Do you eat your school lunches?" I lied. I told her everything I knew she wanted to hear but that she clearly didn't believe. She asked my parents to leave the room, at which point she asked me all the questions again. I broke. I sobbed and told her everything—the whole truth. It felt like I was finally able to open the floodgates of fear, pain, shame, and grief that I had been holding back for years with everything I had. She provided the metaphorical lap for me to climb up into.

My parents joined us in the room again. I was given the diagnosis of anorexia nervosa and something inside felt accomplishment and relief because, in a twisted way, I had achieved my goal. I did it. I was in control; I was enough, and now I could submit that control to people I could trust. I had earned the diagnosis and the right to allow myself to heal. But this was going to take active submission—a daily decision to fight what was comfortable and choose the uncomfortable—in order to achieve real freedom.

It would not be a simple journey, but with God and the support of my treatment team, I could do it. Dr. Portilla told me that had I not been honest and ready to heal, she would have admitted me to the inpatient eating disorder unit immediately. But because she saw I was willing to engage in my recovery, she allowed me to do the outpatient program, which consisted of weekly counseling and medical visits. This would allow me to stay in school and maintain some level of normalcy, which was a huge blessing.

I started eating lunch again; it was by no means substantial. The iceberg lettuce and French dressing were back in rotation, but the important thing was that I was submitting to the act. I was going to fake it until I made it. I would force food until I felt hunger and the natural desire to eat. I was committed, but the need for control was a difficult chain to break. I began drinking gallons of water every day to feel full, especially before weigh-ins, in order to weigh more. I would often do jumping jacks in the school bathroom to burn the extra calories I was now consuming. There were others like me. I knew who they were. They also desired to be invisible. So, when they came into the bathroom for whatever ritual they had developed, we would pass by one another with our eyes and heads down, like skittish cats in a dark alley. Oh, how I wish we had the strength to carry one another, to join forces against the enemy, and to shut him down in our lives. I don't know what came of them, but I pray they now live lives of joy and freedom that Jesus died for them to have.

I worked with a nutritionist as part of my treatment team and was very diligent to follow her guidance. But eating more food and more often made me anxious because the anorexia was a symptom of the anxiety, not the cause. Taking away the control of the food was the only way to truly start digging through the emotional layers to get to the core of what was driving the addiction. I had to feel the pain in my wounds. I did not feel safe in the world, and the constant fear caused by that lack of security needed to be eradicated. I had to break the lies I was believing about myself.

Healing required taking one step, one day at a time, in the right direction, all while giving myself grace on the days I took a step or two back. It required being willing to engage in relationships with others around me so I would not be isolated. It required a surrender of my fear and pain to the Lord, as I held on to the hope of being set free. The Lord had been teaching me how to walk with Him, talk with Him, trust Him, and lean on and into Him by being faithful to show up at every turn. He consistently allowed me to feel His presence and filled me with His peace when I cried out for Him. I had also seen Him answer my prayer by providing the clinic that offered the support team I needed. I was primed and ready for Him to take me to the next level spiritually. He would do it through my counselor, Dr. Smith, who was part of my eating disorder treatment team.

Dr. Smith gave me a safe space to be vulnerable and honest, to identify and give voice to the emotions I was feeling. This man was the first person to teach me spiritual warfare, without saying he was teaching me spiritual warfare. He taught me to identify the voice of "my monster," the "inner critic," in my head. Together, we identified lies I was hearing and believing, and he taught me to take authority over them and to ignore them. Once I had this power, I was a real threat to the plans of the real monster in my life, Satan. I could now identify his lies and cast them down. I also had to recognize that the inner fighter and inner critic in me, who had done such a beautiful job of protecting me over the years, needed to be relieved of their jobs. In order to heal, I needed to allow myself to fail and get back up; I needed to feel my pain; and I needed to allow people to get close.

In the Catholic church, there is a ceremony called confirmation. Confirmation, together with baptism and Eucharist, form the Sacraments of Initiation, and they are all connected. In the Sacrament of Confirmation, you are believed to be sealed with the gift of the Holy Spirit. (I no longer attend a Catholic church; we attend an Evangelical church simply because it is what the Lord has brought me to and I trust His guidance. I have nothing against the Catholic Church. I believe that as long as you are worshiping the One True God and ascribe to the unadulterated Word, He will meet you and strengthen you in your faith.) I needed the Catholic Church in my tenth-grade year, along with my Catholic school, my friends, an encounter with the Holy Spirit, and a move of the hand of *Jehovah Rapha*, "God the Healer." This was all part of God's plan.

I was attending classes at church with a lot of my friends from my elementary school to prepare for our confirmation. It would've been a fun reunion of sorts, but I was still in a battle and embarrassed by how I looked. It was obvious I had taken a turn down the wrong path since they had seen me last. No one said anything mean or even asked questions. I'm sure they had some for my friends, and that was okay. I was pretty open about what I was going through and I had hoped that I would get better and have a future worth living. I was less afraid and less defensive.

I fell to sleep every night in prayer, but it differed from the desperate prayers I used to fall to sleep to where I would beg the Lord to keep my heart pumping while I slept. Even though at the worst point in the eating disorder I wanted to disappear into nothingness, a burden to no one, I never wanted to die. Most of the time, I was afraid that my body could not sustain my life. No, these new prayers were prayers of thanksgiving and repentance, and they were full of hope and a new desperation to be set completely free. I did not want to have to keep battling the enemy all day, every day, in my head, so I asked the Lord to stop him. I needed Him to take away the anxiety that made me want to take control again in unhealthy ways.

This would be the second time in my life that I heard the Lord whisper to me. I was in my bedroom, getting dressed for the confirmation service. I wore a cream long-sleeved shirt under a brown button-down fitted vest with a matching brown knee-length skirt. I had braces at this time, which I hated, and my hair was half pulled up, much thinner than it was before the eating disorder. My older brother was going to be my confirmation sponsor. A sponsor is someone who commits to offering prayerful support and guidance in the Christian walk for the person being confirmed.

I looked up to my brother, and though I know I created a lot of pain, tension, and chaos in the home, he was always a safe place for me. I know he was worried, as was my younger sister, who often stood outside my bedroom door, scared to knock but wanting to so badly. She needed her big sister, and the enemy stole me from her. My younger brother was too young to really understand what was going on but I know for a fact he was affected by the ripples in the family, and for that I will forever be sorry. I pray and trust that the Lord is working in the stories of anyone that my path intersected with and influenced negatively.

So, there I stood, looking in my full-length, wooden-framed oval mirror, when I clearly heard the Lord say, "Accept my Holy Spirit into your heart today, and you will be healed." Of course, I did. I already planned to, but now I could not wait to get to the ceremony. Something incredible happened that day and all the days to follow. It would be a process and would take time, but the enemy was silenced in my mind more and more over time. I didn't drink gallons of water before weigh-ins. I emptied my bladder beforehand because I wanted truth—no more lies, no more being controlled by the enemy.

I wanted only to live in light and to be a person of integrity. As a result, I earned the trust of my medical team, and they released me to exercise again, which was a goal I had been working toward. I had missed the emotional release I felt with movement and I wanted to build physical strength again. My doctors were shocked and overjoyed when I would come in for check-ups, and they noticed I had gained muscle and had a smile on my face. I can't tell you how many days in the past I had gone in with swollen eyes because I cried the whole way there; I was being taken against my will, full of fear and anger. But now, I wanted to go, I wanted to get well, and I wanted them to see that I wasn't so broken after all. I had hope.

"You're like a miracle case," I remember Dr. Smith saying. How right he was. God had proven Himself faithful. I knew I was seen, loved, protected, and cared for by Him.

During the recovery and healing period, God clearly whispered to my spirit, "You are going to counsel other young women like you." At one of my following appointments, Dr. Portilla asked me if I wanted to be a doctor like her. Dr. Smith smiled with pride when I responded, "Nope, I am going to be a counselor like Dr. Smith." Well, joke's on me because I ended up a nurse practitioner, and it wouldn't be until about twelve years later that I would also become a counselor.

I know I took some steps off of the path God had for me even after the miraculous healing, but just as Proverbs 24:16 and Micah 7:8 teach us, we may fall and we may be in the dark, or off course, but God will illuminate our path and help us rise or get back on track. I am living proof that we can't stop His plans for us as long as we continually go back to Him and ask Him to get us back on track. In our surrender to Him, He brings us back to hope, which strengthens and aligns us to keep moving forward. Also, He uses everything for good, and now I have lots of knowledge as a nurse practitioner and counselor that I can share with and sow into clients in various ways, uniquely as God designed.

If you are struggling with an addiction of any sort, I want to encourage you that there is hope. The first step is admitting that there is an issue. I know we hear that all the time, but it's true. God cannot do the healing work if our hearts and spirits are not submitted to Him. It is only by coming to the end of yourself and telling the Lord you are sorry for getting yourself into the mess you are in and that you need Him to take the wheel that He can. He is a God of invitation. He will never force Himself on you. He cannot do the healing work in your heart, mind, and spirit that needs to happen in order for the addiction to be broken if you are still holding on to it and are hiding behind defensiveness.

It's not easy. I'll be the first to tell you that it's hard. It's painful. It will flip your life upside down for a while, but, one day, you will look up and realize you are free and that God is standing next to you, smiling with pride as you continue to step forward in confidence and walk out *your* purpose.

Did you know the enemy can't read your mind, so he doesn't know your thoughts? That brings me so much peace. If you hear his lies, speak truth from the Word out loud for him to hear. Confuse and disarm him. Cry out to the Lord. He is faithful to meet you in the battle and to send the enemy fleeing, just like He did for me. His Word says, "The righteous cry out, and the Lord hears them; He delivers them from all their troubles" (Psalm 34:17). To be righteous means that we live lives that align with the Word of God and that we strive to live like Jesus.

I recommend you find people you trust, whom your spirit feels peace around, and whom you have witnessed living with integrity. Find those who have fruit in their lives that prove they walk with the Lord, the righteous, to walk with you. You may need medical guidance and support from counselors as well. I know I did, and I am so grateful it was available to me. Pray about what your next step should be, with the first being your surrender to the Lord.

I am praying for you.

CHAPTER FIVE
Gaining Confidence

I continued my healing journey, one day at a time, and it would not be without bumps or veering off the path God had for me just a bit. I turned sixteen, and my friends and I got driver's licenses. I forced myself at first to go hang out with friends, to get out of the house, and to try to have some fun. I still lacked self confidence, so when my friend's older sister bought us alcohol, I started drinking to feel less anxious and to fit in. We hung out and drank most weekends and later added in some marijuana. I was the last of my group of friends to try marijuana, and I honestly never liked it. It made me anxious. I would smoke it just to not feel like an outsider but it was not something I craved. I got my braces off, looked healthier, and suddenly boys noticed me. This was all a huge, much-needed confidence boost. I wasn't feeling so different or broken. I was no longer in isolation.

I tried out for the school dance team, The Rockettes, and I made it! I was back to dancing, and I made an entire group of immediate friends. We were close, like a family. Though I turned to things outside of the Lord for comfort and relief, I continued to pursue and speak to Him throughout the day. I would even repent for the things I was doing as I did them. My mom started seeing Dr. Smith for her own counseling, which was healthy for her and the rest of us. I was feeling more peace in our home, which allowed me to feel safe as well. Though I was never one of the bouncy, happy girls, I was starting to walk in the light they danced in as the darkness the enemy had controlled me with was washed away.

A few months later, when I was just about to graduate from the treatment program, the eating disorder clinic started holding support groups. I was still a patient, but I was more of an observer than an active participant and gave feedback on how to better run the group. I offered insight from my perspective as someone in healing on the rules that needed to be established around what should be shared and discussed in the groups. After all, some girls were just stepping into the battle. Many were scared because their control was being threatened and they were there against their will. They were looking for tricks, listening for the weights of other girls so they knew what they had to beat to be enough, or for the rituals of the others that would help them do their eating disorders even better. Many were angry and just wanted to hurt anyone who saw them. They pushed anyone away who wanted them to come out from behind their walls. I knew how they felt, and my heart broke for them. I prayed they would learn spiritual warfare from Dr. Smith and would trust the entire team so they could walk into freedom, too.

I was continuing to make progress in my healing. I was feeling more confident, less anxious, and less broken, and the enemy was no longer holding me captive. Then, one night, my parents asked us to all be home for a family dinner. Mid-bite of my grilled chicken breast, my dad announced we were moving to Tennessee for his job. This was now the middle of my junior year of high school. I had friends. I had my treatment team at the eating disorder clinic. I had my teachers and school. I had my dance team. I had my confidence. This was surely a fiery dart of the enemy—he was mad that he was losing his grip on me.

I was scared, heartbroken, and angry. I had no control over this decision or the outcome. By this point, largely due to the spiritual and emotional healing journey through the eating disorder, I had gotten quite good at submitting control and trusting the Lord because He always showed Himself to be faithful. I eventually accepted that the move was happening and chose to have a positive attitude about it. I believed that God had good plans for the move. I remember one day our dance team was practicing at a football stadium for the halftime performance (at what would be the last football game I would attend with them). I stood in the middle of the field as we lined up for our kick sequence. I looked up at a huge sign advertising Vanderbilt University and felt it was more than just a physical sign. I allowed myself to dream about what could come from this move.

I was also getting weary of the constant partying on the weekends and feeling like I was not honoring my authentic self with the new heart I was developing while walking so closely with the Lord. I was feeling increasingly convicted. I was also acutely aware that the crowd I was running with was dabbling in serious drugs and I knew I would either need to succumb to the pressure and do what I wasn't comfortable with or I would lose my friends. Neither were good options.

I joined my dad in Tennessee one weekend to look at

houses. We laughed as we crawled under garage doors and through the windows of newly built homes after dark. This long overdue quality time gave me hope about what this move may mean for our family. I could see it, as hard as it would be, as a blessing. I would be lying if I said it was easy, that I wasn't grieving most days, anticipating what I would feel when we left town. I would be lying if I said I didn't beg my parents to let me live with Leigha so I could graduate high school in Arkansas with everyone and everything that I knew. I went through the jumbled feelings of denial, anger, bargaining, sadness, and acceptance over and over until the day my bedroom was packed up. The last boxes were being loaded into the moving truck, and Leigha and I sat on my bedroom floor across from one another, her back on one wall and mine on another, sobbing. Staring at one another. No words, just pure, raw grief.

My sister and I drove in my little white Nissan Sentra packed to the roof with our things in what is still, to this day, one of the heaviest thunderstorms I have ever driven in. It was dark out, and I was still a relatively new driver. We could barely see two feet in front of us. It was a miracle we didn't get into a serious accident or cause one. When we got to the family's first meeting spot at a gas station, my mom was in tears because she had been anxious about our driving conditions. There were no cell phones back then, so there was no way my parents could check on us. Honestly, my sister and I were naively oblivious to how dangerous it had been. I just remember pure joy as we danced and sang, "I love it when you call me Big Pa-Pa." We were on a journey to a new beginning together.

Once in Nashville, we stayed in a hotel suite, courtesy of my dad's moving allowance from his job. I remember touring what would be my new school, Father Ryan, another Catholic high school. It was very different from the Mount. This one was co-ed, and clearly the girls cared about how they looked, and, therefore, I would need to as well. I needed to fit in. I wasn't concerned about fitting in to make friends. I guess what I really wanted was the same as when I was the new kid in third grade—to blend in. I wanted to be seen as a normal teen, just like them, and because no one knew my past, this was my chance.

My first day at the new school, I got dressed, did my hair, put on makeup, and drove myself. The drive was a thirty-minute commute on a good day. It was fall, and it was cold. I remember my car wasn't warm until I arrived. I pulled up to the parking lot, carrying the weight of what the day would bring. I was ready to face the unknown. I leaned into the Lord and His strength. I had gotten good at moving forward into situations I had no choice but to enter. It simply required courage for me to forge ahead as I remained in constant communication with the Lord. Together, we crossed over the walking bridge and into the school. My plan was to just survive and exist for the next year and a half until I could move back to Arkansas to be with my friends. That took the pressure off me. I just needed to make it through. I didn't need to gain friends or impress anyone.

God did something for me that first day of school that was so sweet, so amazing, and something only a truly loving Father would do. He prepared for me a friend, or as the school called her, my "buddy," to show me around. Gina is still one of my best friends today. I don't know if she intended for me to hang around every day past that first day, but I did. She had no expectations of me. Gina was accepting, friendly, safe, and patient with me. After introducing me to her friends, they took me in as well. It was an incredible example of God's love and provision.

I was again enrolled in all AP classes, but they were less rigorous and academically challenging than the ones at the Mount. There was something about the co-ed atmosphere that made everything more laid back. I couldn't help but think that maybe this type of school would've been the better option for me from the beginning. Despite the curriculum being less rigorous, I still struggled because they were in the middle of lessons that we were not learning at the Mount. We were covering different material, and this forced me to accept that I could no longer earn perfect grades if I wanted to maintain whatever level of internal peace I had gained and not go backward in my healing journey. I did the best I could and accepted when my best didn't result in all A's.

Deuteronomy 31:8 says, "The Lord Himself goes before you and will be with you; He will never leave you or forsake you... God will go before you and come behind you." This was true of my experience with this move. God had gone before me and provided everything I needed. At Father Ryan, I was a new girl, awkward and guarded, who stepped into a group of friends who were nothing but kind. They were also more aligned with the new heart God had been weaving in me. They did not drink, smoke, or do drugs. They did fun things like bowling and met up at parks to run. I joined the cross country team again, with my new friends, this time in a healthy headspace. I was no longer running to feel pain; I wanted to feel my strength.

We all have times of transition and uncertainty in our lives, and the only comfort we can truly know is that of knowing beyond the shadow of a doubt that God truly never leaves us. As God says in Isaiah 43:2, "When you pass through the waters, I will be with you; and when you pass through the rivers, they will not sweep over you. When you walk through the fire, you will not be burned; the flames will not set you ablaze."

You see, the Lord already knows what is coming because He is already there. He is not confined by space or time. Nothing that happens in our lives is a surprise to Him. As long as we ask Him to be with us and to make a way for us, we can trust in Him as we walk it out. Ask the Lord to lead you, protect you, and provide for you along your journey; He is faithful to do it, and you are never alone.

CHAPTER SIX
Learning the Realities of Love and Life

One day during my second week at the new school, I was walking to class through a busy hallway lined with windows. I looked up just in time to lock eyes with a tall, olive-skinned boy with dark brown ringlet curls hanging over his forehead. He was wearing a blue button-down shirt and a cool, unique tie that looked like he may have discovered it in a vintage store, or maybe Goodwill. I wanted to look away immediately because I felt as if his eyes were saying he would uncover everything I had hidden from the world—things I had hidden from myself. He gave me a sideways smile as the sunlight bounced off of his green eyes. We passed, and with butterflies in my stomach and legs unsteady, I walked to my next class. I asked my friend who he was. She told me his name (which was, of course, as unique as he was) and that he had a girlfriend. *Phew,* crisis averted, pressure off. I could stay hidden while I crushed on him.

That was until a few weeks later when I was resting on my backpack in the hall before school. He tapped me on the shoulder and asked if he could talk to me. I followed him to a more private part of the hall. Flustered, he said he wanted to take me out but that he had a girlfriend. It felt like an apology. I was confused, as it seemed as if he was responding to a request I never made. Looking into his intense eyes, I told him it was okay, and we parted ways. It felt good to know he saw me and was interested. I knew we would find our way to one another. I could feel it; we had a connection.

About a week later, he broke up with his girlfriend and invited me to watch a basketball game with him one night at the school. We watched for about one minute before we walked the track outside to talk, which we did for the remainder of the game. He called me that night, and we continued to talk until the sun came up. He was easy to talk to. I normally hated talking on the phone, but I never wanted to hang up with him.

I remember going to his house early in our "getting to know one another" period and listening to music in his room. He loved music as much as I did. He played Mr. Big's "To Be With You." I requested that he play it again and again. I wanted those lyrics to be true of him. I wanted him to keep looking at me the way he did in the hall that day, to keep pursuing me freely with no games. He did. Ready or not, he pursued me unapologetically.

Eventually, he rode with me to and from school, which meant we saw a lot of one another. When I would get consumed by stress, I would sit next to him in the car, silent and eyes forward, trying to go back inside myself as I used to when I felt overwhelmed. He knew what to do to draw me away from my thoughts. Most of the time, this looked like him staring at me until I couldn't ignore him, or spitting water at me to get my attention, and then, as my eyes met his, I couldn't help but smile, and the walls would come down. He seemed to fall fast and hard, and I fell just as hard, but I was apprehensive. I was not as quick to let others in.

He was an incredible person. He had tons of friends. He was a Christian. He was an artist. He didn't know how broken I had been, and the enemy reminded me often that I didn't deserve him. This made me doubt his feelings for me and pull away. Inevitably, I would break up with him more than once. We would get back together, and each time he took me back, I trusted my own judgment less and felt shame for hurting him and for being wishy-washy. The cycle would continue as we moved on to college, but the summer before, we were hopeful that we would have much more time together living in a co-ed dorm. We would be going to the University of Tennessee, Knoxville (UTK), near the Smoky Mountains, and were excited about taking day trips to hike when we needed to escape campus life, decompress, and spend quality time together.

In the fall of 1997, we all went off to UTK. Gina became my roommate and workout partner. We ran around the campus at 5 o'clock every morning—rain, sleet, or snow (literally, and sometimes all at once). My diet consisted of steamed rice and cafeteria salads. I wasn't restricting; there just weren't great food choices and eating healthy was a priority for me. I wasn't getting adequate sleep. I got frequent sinus infections (pretty sure we had mold in our dorm) and would take antibiotics to press on. All of that to say, I had extra stress emotionally with the transition from home to dorm life, as well as physically. My immune system was fighting an uphill battle to keep me well, and I could never have predicted what would happen next.

I had my wisdom teeth removed during the Christmas

break of my freshman year. The surgery seemed to be pretty straightforward as far as minor surgeries go, except I remember I was terrified of being "put under" for fear I would not wake up. During surgery, I dreamt I was trying to pray the Lord's prayer (Matt. 6:9-10) and couldn't remember the words. At one point, I looked at the nurse, and she looked back at me with wide eyes.

"You're awake," she said before she scrambled to get more sedative. The next thing I knew, I was waking up to the sounds of my mom and the surgeon talking. Thank God I had survived the surgery, and thank God my mom didn't have a cell phone with which to record me after my surgery, ha. All seemed to have gone well, but what I didn't know at the time was the hell the surgery unleashed into my bloodstream.

I napped on and off that day with ice packs strapped to my cheeks. My mouth was healing up just fine, but the morning after the surgery, I woke up with a few red nodules on my legs. I called the surgeon's office, letting him know, and was told it could just be an allergic reaction to medication. I accepted their explanation, and, feeling well enough, I went on with my normal routine and went for a run. The nodules were round, red, painful lumps ranging from the size of a pea to a golf ball just under my skin. When they went away, they looked like big red circles and then bruises. This was the first of what would be many flares I would experience moving forward.

By the second semester of freshman year, I could feel my boyfriend pulling away. He was in the art department and was meeting cool, artsy girls who had a lot in common with him and wanted him for themselves. I did not blame them —of course they did. I felt like he deserved them. I just knew one of those lighthearted, fun girls would be what he needed. I was also worn out physically, emotionally, and mentally from my first year in college and all it brought, so, without the pressure of a relationship on me, I could have a summer to breathe. We agreed that we should take a break, at least for a few months. I was excited to rest and spend time with my sister, whom I had grown very close to since we moved to Tennessee, and my friends.

I went into my sophomore year of college single. I chopped my hair and wanted an all-around fresh start. I spent more time with friends, enjoyed school, and went out to dance clubs on the weekends. One of my friends was a DJ, and he would play my song, my anthem for that season, "Feeling So Good" by Jennifer Lopez, when he saw me walk into the club. Gina and I moved into an apartment on campus, and in a painful twist of fate, so did my ex-boyfriend, and his bedroom was across the courtyard from mine. I could sit in my room and see into his, and I knew he could see me, too. I wanted to run to him every day, but I did not allow myself to. I missed him but felt I needed to be alone to continue working on my emotional healing to understand who I was becoming and what God had planned for me. Eventually, we did start hanging out again in the same friend group, and, of course, we ended up back together.

About six months later, I stayed on campus for summer classes, and he went back home to work. I was feeling overwhelmed with work (waiting tables) and school, I felt emotionally vulnerable and unsettled in our relationship being apart for the summer. I missed him horribly and needed his lighthearted presence and reassurance.

It was right about this time that the nodules flared up

more and more often, now not just in my legs but in my arms as well. Eventually, fevers, sweats, brain fog, joint pain, and debilitating headaches would accompany them. The flares would come on somewhat slowly, with a nodule here or there, warning me to brace myself. The worst part of the flare was the full cluster of symptoms and high fevers that would typically last a week, and then I would begin the recovery phase. From the first nodule to the resolution of the bruises, a full flare usually lasted about a month. At the worst times, I would have them back-to-back, so I would be recovering from one just as another was starting. The doctors told me all I could do was go on bed rest, take ibuprofen, and put ice packs on my legs. Other than when I was delirious with fever, I did not stay in bed. If this was something I had to live with, I would live with it, not lie in bed while it stole the life I had already fought so hard to keep.

No one, not even my boyfriend or Gina, really knew what I was going through because I didn't want anyone worrying about me. My parents didn't understand the full extent of what was happening because I didn't live at home, so they didn't witness the flares. I had to face this thing alone. Having unclear "answers" from the doctors, all I knew to do was carry on as best I could and press harder into the Lord, reminding Him that I trusted Him as my healer.

My boyfriend could feel me pulling away, as was still my coping mechanism when I was afraid or stressed. So he came to visit me one weekend, and with hope bigger than perspective, he proposed. I remember feeling like he asked out of fear of losing me and because he felt it was expected of him, not from a place of sincerity, strength, or a true understanding of what it meant to commit to a life together and all that would entail, especially with me and this mystery illness. I know that is also what I was feeling when I said "yes." My heart said yes but my spirit said, "Karen, what did you do?" I did not have peace about it. It didn't feel like it was our time, largely because I felt like I was still stumbling and trying to get my footing in so many areas, and I did not want to hurt him.

In the fall, I moved into an apartment off campus because I wanted to get away from as many distractions as I could. I needed to focus and graduate. The campus was a busy place; I desired a reset and some down time. My boyfriend, now fiancé, eventually moved in with me because we spent all our time together anyway. I often felt suffocated when he wanted to spend every minute with me in the apartment, and I needed alone time to read, write, workout, or just relax. But then I was insecure when he would spend time away in the darkroom developing his photos and attending parties with his art friends.

It was a time of uncertainty, and I felt like we were trying to force the relationship to work. I prayed that God would shut the door if it wasn't meant to be. I didn't want to make a mistake if we were destined to be together forever. God would have to show up. I also needed to hear from my fiancé what he wanted, even if it meant he didn't want me. One night, as we sat at our dining room table with silence between us, I could tell he was fighting himself to get the words out that needed to be said. When he finally did, he broke up with me and did it as gently as possible. I was proud of him. It was painful, but I had been praying for clarity and I knew deep down it was best. I also now know that pushing people away was a protective coping mechanism for me, so though my heart was broken, I felt relieved.

Often, those who face a prolonged illness feel broken and like they no longer have value. It's easy to feel like no one truly knows what you are experiencing, and it can negatively affect your relationships if you don't at least try to be vulnerable and share your hardships; I admittedly was not great at this. There are also some people who may find it to be too much and will abandon you. But those aren't your people, and there are always those who find meaning and their life's purpose in coming alongside those who are suffering. There are people who see your value in just being the beautiful creation that you are. If you are living with an illness, pray for God to bring these people into your life.

I have worked with many patients for whom the healing on this side of heaven didn't come. It is difficult to live with something in your life that is a constant reminder of your own humanity and frailty, but what I have landed on by walking through my own is that I am grateful for the thorn God has allowed in my life. I can tell you I would not be living with the peace and emotional and spiritual maturity I am if I had not been desperate for the Lord in my health since I was a teenager. I truly overcame any remnants of the eating disorder right as the mystery illness developed with the removal of my wisdom teeth. Dealing with illness—especially when no one has answers for you—can be isolating in its own way and oddly shame-inducing, because at times you wonder if there is something wrong with you, if God abandoned and forgot you.

Continue to invite God into your fight every day and at every doctor appointment. Lay every symptom at His feet. Sit in His peace as you get tests and reports, and continue to pray for and claim His healing. By His stripes, you have been healed (Isaiah 53:5). You have been washed in His blood and living water. If you surrender to Christ through your suffering, it doesn't always mean the suffering ceases immediately; it often means that the Holy Spirit will sustain you in the waiting. Through your suffering, the character of Jesus can be formed in you. That means that through your suffering, you can share in Jesus' glory by being transformed by His grace and truth (Romans 8:15-28).

CHAPTER SEVEN
First Heartbreak

Even though my heart was prepared and I knew it was best for us, or so I convinced myself, the days, weeks, and months following our breakup brought groans of sadness from the deepest parts of me. I had to elicit the strength of the Holy Spirit every day, multiple times a day, to keep me from running back to my now ex. He showed up at the apartment saying we had made a mistake a few times, and I had to shut down every natural urge I had welling up in me to wrap myself in his love. In order to say "no," I felt I had to be the strong one.

Spring break was a few weeks after our breakup, and I went to Arkansas. I went camping with Leigha, her boyfriend, and his friends. There was someone she wanted me to meet but I was not ready, and I can say with full confidence that he wasn't either.

After spring break, I decided to move back to Arkansas as originally planned when we moved to Tennessee as a family a few years prior. I would move in with Leigha and finish school at the University of Central Arkansas (UCA) with a major in writing and a minor in theater. I don't know how I talked my parents into being on board with this plan, but they supported me. I believed it was another opportunity to explore new beginnings and align with what I truly wanted to do. I also knew if I stayed at the University of Tennessee, I would not remain strong enough to turn my ex away or keep from running to him. The strength it took for me to move away was drawn from the vision and hope of a life we may be able to have together one day or the dream of meeting someone else with whom I could build a life. Ultimately, what I really wanted was for my ex to be happy, and I wanted to be happy, too.

The day before I was to leave town, he asked me to spend time with him. We hiked, talked, and went by the liquor store on the way to my apartment—the apartment that once housed our relationship and life together. We talked over some drinks. We laughed and cried, probably sharing more openly about our experiences being together and the feelings involved than we ever had before. This interaction was a step in the right direction toward healing for both of us. This time together allowed for apologies and forgiveness. We had inevitably hurt one another in our relationship, even though we hadn't intended to. We were young and had done the best we could with the tools we had.

Since we had been drinking, he stayed the night. I went to the bedroom and shut the door. He went to the couch. I did not sleep at all that night. I fought the desire to go curl up in his arms, saying, "It's okay. We can be together; we will figure it out." Instead, I put Alison Krauss' album, *Forget About It*, on repeat, volume low so he couldn't hear. The album had been my companion in my grief for months. Her words washed over me as I cried quietly and wondered what he was thinking; I would never know.

I am truly grateful for the relationship I had during these years. He was kind, funny, and my best friend. I learned to be vulnerable. I felt that he truly liked who I was and loved me just as I was. He didn't require makeup or for me to pretend I was anything other than the real, often emotional, often guarded, but also quirky, funny, and smart girl he called his during this time. I loved who he was and that he felt comfortable being himself and being vulnerable with me as well.

I think young love is so powerful in our lives because we are still becoming who we are meant to be. The person you are with during this time, if healthy for you, makes that process much easier and can help instill confidence in you that you will carry for the rest of your life. So, though first loves rarely last, the impact they have on us can be lifelong. My first love showed me I deserved to be loved well and, inspired by the words of Rory Gilmore, as much as I may have wished over the years that I had met him when I was older and more mature, he "taught me what safe feels like." For that I will forever be grateful.

I know many people who also have positive first love experiences and some who have very painful experiences. I pray that you will only take from yours what is healthy and leave behind anything that does not edify and build you up, reminding you that you are the child of the One True King. God loves you just as you are because, through Jesus, we are all His children by faith (Romans 8:15), and He created you!

Another powerful practice is to pray that the Lord will break the soul ties you have with anyone in your past who may still have some sort of emotional or spiritual hold in your life. There are several verses referring to soul ties; one example of a godly soul tie is marriage: "For this reason a man will leave his father and mother, and be united to his wife, and the two will become one flesh, so they are no longer two, but one flesh" (Mark 10:7-8). If this is new for you, I encourage you to dig into the Word and what God says about soul ties; He will lead you.

CHAPTER EIGHT
New Beginnings

Remarkably, through the heightened emotions of the breakup and the move, I stayed quite healthy. The engagement was called off, goodbyes were said, and moving day was upon me. My parents met me at my apartment with a moving truck and helped me pack up all of my things in Tennessee. We intended to sell or store what we could, but we all felt a bit overwhelmed and felt like a fresh start was in order. My dad and I took a truck full to Goodwill and were done with it.

I went home for only a few days of respite and time with my family before I embarked on the next chapter of my young adult life. I was excited about the unknown. I knew that whenever there was change, there was an opportunity for God to work. I was inviting Him in to do whatever He wanted, and I couldn't wait to see what was in store.

After a six-hour solo road trip, one I had done many times in high school to see Leigha in Arkansas since we moved, I pulled up to her townhouse. This would be my new home. It looked like she was throwing a party. I felt honored, but I would soon learn this was just what they did. Leigha, her boyfriend, and their friends drank and hung out every weekend, and often on weeknights, too. Not much different from the scene I left in high school, just now without curfews. It was a sort of relief; I needed to disconnect and have lighthearted fun.

I got out of my car and was met by the boy my friend had wanted me to meet, the one I met briefly on the camping trip during spring break. He was the one I was not ready for, and he was most definitely not ready for me. His name was Matt. He was tall and handsome with blue eyes, dark hair, and sun-kissed skin. He opened my door and inquired about how my trip had gone. Matt went out of his way to make me feel welcome, earning immediate points in my book. Throughout the night, he would catch my eye, give me a smile, and check on me to see if I needed anything. Then, reserved and mysterious, he would be gone again.

Only a few months out of my serious relationship when I arrived in Arkansas, I was surprised when Matt moved in for a kiss the very first night. However, I was intrigued by him, and having been lonely and heartbroken since my breakup, I was excited when he called me the next morning to go to the lake with him and some of his friends. I appreciated that he did not play games or make me wonder what his intentions were. He was interested in me, and I was interested in him.

Over the next few days, I was introduced to those who would eventually become my new friend group. They were nice and welcoming, but I didn't have much in common with them. As much as I loved reuniting with Leigha, we would've maintained a friendship no matter where I was. I have often wondered what would've happened if I moved somewhere completely new where no one knew me—where the future was wide open, a blank canvas for God to work on. Just God and me on an adventure. But I didn't. I moved back to Arkansas. I started to wonder if maybe Matt was the reason I felt I needed to move there; maybe he was the one I was meant to build a life with.

I finally had a major in college that I could be passionate about: writing. At UTK, I was all over the place. I wanted to do everything and had no direction. I started out pre-med, then dabbled in dance, theater, and art, with some writing and psychology dribbled into my schedule. For someone like me who wanted to know, do, and understand many things, a large campus with little direction was not a good situation. This smaller school in Arkansas, UCA, was a good place for me to focus and graduate.

I tried to create some healthy new beginnings for myself. I had a new boldness about me. I had made new friends and had a new love interest. Minoring in theater, the boldness translated into me trying out for a traveling children's theater troupe. The tryout consisted of me choreographing a dance and then performing it in a small room for the theater director, who was seated at a table in front of me, with other theater students watching. It was an awkward situation and took courage as well as humility. I had been advised by other professors at UTK that I should do film acting instead of theater because my voice didn't carry, but this theater director gave me a chance. Not only did I get a spot in the troupe, but I made great friends who were lights in my life during this season. I don't know that I have ever laughed so hard, so consistently, as I did with that group of creatives. I also got a job at a pizza place, so I had money, and I volunteered at an adults-with-disabilities center.

Despite my best efforts to pursue the healthy new path I

knew God had for me, the saying "You become who you hang out with" is true. Eventually I found myself giving in to hanging out and drinking with Leigha and her friends, including Matt, more and more. They were always at our townhouse or were hanging out at Matt's house, which is where I was when I wasn't home. I was bored and frustrated most of the time. I was definitely not on the path God had for me, and I felt stuck. I wanted so much more for my life. I felt like I had taken ten steps backward. It was no one's fault but my own. They were all hard-working college students who were just enjoying their downtime. I had not yet learned how to do that without feeling guilty about it. So, I started second-guessing myself and resenting my situation.

The resentment and boredom took a toll on my new relationship. I wasn't happy. Our physical connection was one of the strongest parts of our relationship, and it was becoming clear that it was one of the only ways we were connecting.

The way we communicated was also very different, especially in conflict. Matt was a fighter, which was new to me. Before him, I don't know that I had ever raised my voice at anyone. I had wanted to, but I just never had. I never saw my parents fight, and I hadn't fought in previous relationships. It was, however, what Matt was used to, and every time he got loud to make his point (at 6'5" with an already booming voice, his loud was *extra* loud), I would shut down and shut him out, so we never really resolved anything. This happened often and resulted in a tumultuous dating life.

Though I did not feel suffocated like I sometimes did in my previous relationship because I had plenty of time to myself when he was at work or with his friends, this new relationship felt unstable. I felt rejected a lot of the time because his friends seemed to take priority. It was as if he wanted me to be his girlfriend but resented me for expecting him to act like my boyfriend. I also had expectations that were not communicated and were potentially unrealistic in such a new relationship. He was still healing from his parents' divorce that had only happened a few years before we met, and he did not speak of it much. Feeling lost and broken, he was not quite ready to be vulnerable or trust me with his heart. Though I can look back now and understand the dynamics at play, and he and I can now discuss issues and understand each other much better (hindsight is always 20/20, right?), at the time I just felt confused, abandoned, disappointed, and angry.

During this time, my ex and I would speak on and off. He was dating—a lot—and I remember feeling like he was doing better without me. There were always some sentiments of "what if" and "maybe one day" that kept a vision for us alive in my heart, especially when I didn't feel confident in my relationship with Matt. So, one trip home, as I was craving the safety and comfort of the relationship with my ex, we let our guards down and had one last night together. We knew we had made a mistake; if there would ever be a time for us to be back together, that wasn't it. We were both working to find our footing without one another and needed to keep exploring our paths.

I was honest with Matt and immediately broke up with him because I thought for sure I had ruined any chance we had. He was already having a hard time trusting me and being vulnerable. I was mad at myself for wrecking our relationship and hated that I hurt him. I will say that I was shocked at how hurt he was. It was as if we were in two different relationships. In his mind, we were much more serious and healthier than in reality. I had broken his heart when, honestly, I didn't even know I was holding it.

Not long after, in my second year in Arkansas, I moved into my own apartment. I was working as a leasing agent, getting closer to graduating, and newly attending a Catholic church. I was also volunteering to teach CCD classes for kids, like the ones I attended in my younger years.

The flares were increasing in severity and worse than ever before. I sought the help of different specialists, and none had any better answers or guidance than another. I am not someone who is okay with not having answers, so you can understand the frustration in receiving the diagnosis "erythema nodosum," which literally translates to redness or inflammation with no known cause. This thing that was attacking me, that had no known cause, was diagnosed as an autoimmune disorder, but we will find out later that it was not the entire story, or even an accurate one.

I wasn't able to get help from primary care, dermatology, rheumatology, or gynecology. I once took myself to the ER because I had a headache that would not subside, and I was scared. I baffled everyone. I had doctors bring textbooks into my exam room so they could read case studies to me. As they showed me pictures from the books, they would say things like, "Did you know you could have these nodules in your brain?" They found it fascinating, but I found it terrifying. My headache was so painful, I was sure they were right and could only imagine the damage it was doing to my brain.

My rheumatologist (the doctor you get sent to when you've been diagnosed with an autoimmune disorder) didn't know what to do for me. He didn't know what was causing the flares, so he didn't know how to help me heal.

His goal was just to manage the symptoms. He would often prescribe high doses of steroids. They would clear the flare, but I would have a rebound flare as soon as the steroids were gone. All anyone could tell me was that the source was stress. So, then I was stressed about my stress, and the cycle continued. It was clear I would need to find answers and advocate for myself as I followed God's lead. You will see in the rest of my story that He would be faithful to provide, but outside of Him, I felt very alone in the battle.

Matt and I ran in the same friend group, so we spent lots of time together. The same draw toward one another that we had when I first moved was still strong. He said he forgave me for the night with my ex, and we ended up dating again. During this time, though I was not walking the Christian walk I walk today, I was feeling closer to the Lord. I was desperate for Him, and just like the anorexia, being isolated in the physical illness and flares with the Lord was like a pressure cooker for my faith. I started to feel shame about the fact that Matt and I were sexually active and not married. I knew I could not fully experience the presence of the Holy Spirit while living in sin. I also really started to value our relationship and wanted us to have a new, healthy start.

We talked about a future, and I had hoped we were truly building a life together. I finally felt safe in our relationship and started letting my walls come down. I was committed; he was the one. Then one Sunday, my church brought in a dynamic speaker who spoke about reclaiming your virginity. I had a fire in my belly and was so excited to reclaim my purity and be forgiven so that I could walk forward in confidence and set healthy boundaries in our relationship for the first time. This was probably one piece I so desperately needed for my healing. Before that, I put little value on my sexuality and didn't feel I was someone worth waiting for. I had given up my virginity shortly before we moved in highschool to someone I had no feelings for. I believed that because I didn't love him, he would not have the power to hurt me. I did not want anyone to have that power. I am not sure where that rationalization based on fear came from, but it was a lie.

So, after church, I went back to my apartment to wake Matt and tell him my newfound revelation and how it would bring new life and emotional and spiritual connection into our relationship. This came out of nowhere for him. I had only just started to be more vulnerable with him and share emotionally. Also, my time with the Lord was private; our faith was not something we discussed. He didn't know how I had been growing spiritually. That is, until I came in like a hurricane, excited and talking about shifting the entire dynamic of our relationship.

He looked at me like I was someone he'd never met before, like I was crazy. He pulled me close into his strong arms, my favorite place to be, and said, "But, we already do it." I felt in that moment that I was probably being ridiculous. All of our friends were living the same lifestyle, so I felt how awkward my request must have been. I knew choosing the way of God over the way of the world was always the better choice, but I was scared that I might lose Matt if I pushed the subject.

The roaring fire in my belly went quickly to a pile of cinders. The enemy used how he responded to validate in my mind the belief that my sexuality was of no value. I felt embarrassed and ashamed for even discussing it with Matt. I stuffed my emotions and we carried on as we were. What I didn't know at this time was that though he told me he forgave me, he still harbored resentment toward me about my ex. He didn't trust that I wouldn't try to leave him again, so I wasn't the only one he was sleeping with at that time.

This is an impactful part of my story because, as it comes to light later, it will not only threaten to take me down, but our family as well. Betrayals had started a thread of distrust and resentment that would be woven into most of our life moving forward and would be something we would have to work together to break.

It's possible that God sending the speaker wasn't just for me, and that I was meant to share it with you right now, where you are, through my story. You can reclaim your virginity or confess any sin or shame you carry. It's not crazy. Jesus died for our sins, and just as Isaiah 1:18 says, "Though your sins are like scarlet, they shall be as white as snow; though they are red as crimson, they shall be like wool." God sees you, loves you, and values you. Follow your heart and heed your peace. His plans for you are always good, so you can trust Him when He leads you to do something that others may think is "crazy."

Follow Him, and you will grow closer to Him as your feet are bound to the paths He laid for you. Choosing to walk the narrow, less traveled path, comes with the greatest blessings and keeps you tucked into God's protection. The path Matt and I would walk moving forward, because we didn't choose to go God's way, has not kept us from His plans for us but has allowed obstacles and pain along the way that were not part of God's plan. Even so, God has met us in them and has sustained and redeemed us. He will do the same for you.

CHAPTER NINE
A Rocky Start

I realized it was an unrealistic expectation that Matt would excitedly jump on board when I suggested we reclaim our virginity and have boundaries around physical intimacy in our relationship, so I was embarrassed. I was also disappointed, but I had been falling in love with him and wanted to continue to hold on to hope for a path forward for us. My walls continued to come down, we were communicating better and more effectively, and he was even teaching me how to rest without feeling guilty. I was enjoying the downtime we spent together with our friends instead of resenting it and feeling stuck.

About two months later, I went home for Christmas break with my family. I always looked forward to going home to see my younger siblings. My older brother had started his own life in Arkansas and no longer lived at home. My parents had become more relaxed and seemed happier as we got older, and they and their marriage matured. My dad traveled far less, if ever; Mom was much more at ease, and both were much easier to be around. There was a lot less tension. I knew God was working in them and their relationship, and home was feeling more like a safe respite for me.

During this visit, I felt a bit "off" physically. I would stand and stare into an open refrigerator because, though I was hungry, there was nothing I wanted to eat. I noticed that my normal runs through the neighborhood were more difficult for me to push through, and I felt exhausted all the time. My mom laughed at my odd behavior in the kitchen and joked, "Are you pregnant?" Then I realized I had missed a period.

Since I recovered from the eating disorder, I regained my menstrual cycle, but periods were never regular, so it didn't cause alarm if I missed one. We were also diligent, *most* of the time, to use various forms of pregnancy prevention. My sister wanted me to take a pregnancy test, but I wanted to wait until I got home if my period had not started by then. I felt sure I wasn't pregnant. To be safe, I called my gynecologist, who prescribed a progesterone challenge to see if my period just needed a jump start.

When I returned to Arkansas, I had finished the progesterone challenge and had no period. By now, I was also experiencing some nausea in the mornings. I went to the drugstore and bought three pregnancy tests. Alone in my apartment, I took them all, and all were positive immediately. It didn't feel real. I thought, *This has to be a mistake,* and *Do I even want to have kids?* I had not thought that far ahead.

Matt showed up and heard me crying. He met me in the bathroom and was calm and supportive. I think he was also thinking the tests were wrong. I had not given him any sort of heads-up. I don't think he even knew I had missed a period. It's fair to say we may have both been in shock. So, we went back to the drugstore and bought about six more tests. All were positive immediately. No more denying it; we were pregnant.

It turned out that around the time the speaker came to my church to discuss reclaiming virginity was when we conceived our daughter, Ava. Let me be *very* clear here: Ava was not a mistake. Ava is the result of God's faithfulness in answering my cries of desperation for Him to forgive me for not valuing what He valued and for not trusting Him in my story by setting a boundary and submitting the outcome of my relationship to Him. Ava is ultimately the epitome of God using everything for my good. He took my sin, the lies I was believing, and my shame; He replaced them all with forgiveness, healing, and a daughter who would be nothing less than God's love and light personified. She is an answer to prayer, not the result of sin.

The first thing Matt said after confirming that we were pregnant was that we should get married. To which I responded, "Take some time to be sure that's what you really want. I don't want you marrying me just because I am pregnant." What I really wanted to say was, "Please love me, choose me, tell me I am safe, and that you'll do what it takes to be a wonderful dad and husband. Tell me I am worth loving and protecting, and that you are the one who wants to do it. Tell me you are going to change your ways." But deep down I didn't believe I deserved it.

I was also scared and ashamed and knew that what I really hoped he could provide, he couldn't, at least not then. I knew we were not yet a healthy couple. We still had lots of growing and maturing to do in ourselves and in our relationship. I wanted to make it work with him, and our future had just taken a sharp turn into unknown territory, so moving forward with him was a better option than moving home and doing it without him. Ultimately, it was no longer about me anyway. It was about this miracle baby and making sure she had the healthiest start and home life I could provide for her, which I was determined to do.

So, there I was, twenty-three years old, pregnant, unwed, and feeling more broken than ever. I withdrew from my position as a CCD teacher at church. After all, I would not be a good example for the children, and I felt sure I would meet the judgmental looks of the parents, or maybe just sympathy; either way, I was not strong enough for that. I was, however, brave enough to go to a face-to-face confession, to look the priest in the eyes as I repented with no screen to hide behind. I will never forget as, through tears, I confessed my sin that I was pregnant out of wedlock and that I had succumbed to fear and shame. I braced myself for his response, his disappointment, and his judgment, but the priest looked at me with both compassion and frustration.

"Who told you your life would be a fairytale?" I did not expect that response. I felt relieved because he didn't tell me I was going to hell, but also kind of sad. I guess I always held hope that there may be a happily ever after possible for me. He gave me a few Hail Marys to pray and sent me back out into the church, where I ran into Dr. Portilla from my eating disorder treatment team years ago. I thought, *If only she knew what a "miracle case" I was now.* Tail between my legs, head down, I stopped going to church after that day, but I didn't stop pressing in with the Lord—more desperately now than ever. I had not imagined a baby in my life until I found out I was pregnant, and then it felt as if it was always meant to be. I would need the Lord through it all, especially to help me be a good mom.

Matt and I had love and support from our parents and family after the initial shock of it all wore off. With his grandmother's ring that his mother gifted us, Matt proposed a few months later. I wish I could tell you we have a beautiful engagement story like we see all over social media nowadays where my nails were done, with our family and friends gathered to capture it on film and video, and that he pondered and planned it for months. I know you're not surprised to hear that this is not our story, and I can honestly say now that I am okay with how it really happened... Super Bowl Sunday. It was after a fight and in desperation to keep me—not because I think he was in love with me but because he was scared. He left me in sobs and quickly went to his car to retrieve the engagement ring he'd had in his glove compartment for weeks because he knew in this moment that I was so angry and frustrated that I was only a few breaths away from telling him I would raise our daughter on my own, and mean it.

I don't know if getting engaged was what he wanted or what I wanted, but I believe we thought it was, and we felt it was the right thing to do. The good news is that this is only part of our story, and if I expected a post-worthy engagement story to come from a place of such brokenness, that would be on me. It would be incredibly unrealistic.

In full transparency, there were many years that I would reflect on this event and kick myself for ever saying yes. The enemy would beat me up with it every time we had a challenge. But now I can look back and see the larger picture; I can see how and when the enemy tried to tear us apart. I thank God for those two kids who were brave enough to chase love and a healthy family even though they didn't believe they were worthy and didn't know what they were doing or what they were in for.

I look back now and can see God's protection in sending a speaker to remind me of my worth in His eyes and to convict me because if I had heeded the message and set a boundary, maybe Matt would've left me and I would've found out about the cheating. And though it would've hurt, it would've saved me from years of hurt. However, if this outcome meant I wouldn't have our children in my life, I would never want it. (I say "if" because I like to think they would've been mine at some point, with someone, no matter what. None of us knows for sure, so I choose to believe that.)

Another possibility I think about is that maybe if I had set the boundary, Matt would've moved toward healing with me, and we would've grown closer. All that was in darkness would've come to light, and the enemy would've no longer had a foothold in our relationship. We would have truly forgiven one another and we would have had healing and a firm foundation on which to start our marriage; we still would have had Ava, just in a much healthier home. I want to warn that while entertaining "what ifs" in our stories is a normal part of processing pain, regret, and grief, we have to be careful to ultimately land not in regret but in being content to not know alternate outcomes. We have to truly trust God with His plans and our future. We know suffering, or challenges, produces perseverance—perseverance, character, and hope. There is always hope as long as we invite God into our circumstances.

If you find yourself in an unplanned pregnancy, I know how scary that can feel. Again, it is an opportunity for the enemy to attempt to get you into isolation. However, it is now that you will need community more than ever. It is now that you will need people who offer love, encouragement, and support. I drove past a billboard one day where the message implied that the only way the woman pictured was able to go to school and pursue a career was because she had an abortion. Well, that is clearly a lie. Children are a blessing. Is there responsibility and financial means that are necessary to care for a child? Yes. Is adoption an option if you feel you are unable or ill-equipped to care for and raise a child? Also, yes.

It breaks my heart to think of all of the incredible people and the calls on their lives that were hijacked by the fear and lies of the enemy. I *never* thought about not keeping Ava. I knew it would be challenging given our relationship and lack of finances, but it was never a question for either of us. And it certainly has not stopped me from pursuing and achieving all of the desires God has placed in my heart for my life. I did not have anyone come and raise her or pay our bills or my tuition. We did not have a trust fund to pay for her college. No, all we had was faith that God would provide and would bless the work of our hands, and He always has.

We are not special. He promises to "meet all your needs" (Philippians 4:19). I am not going to lie and tell you the path is always easy, but it is doable, and it's another opportunity to surrender to the Lord, to let Him show up and show off. The joy of the Lord will be your strength; trust Him and take one step of faith at a time (Nehemiah 8:10).

If you have had an abortion, hear me… there is no condemnation in Christ Jesus (Romans 8:1-3). You are forgiven, and God grieves with you. I have walked with women and men through the sadness they have felt about an abortion. We all have things in our lives that grieve our spirits, things we would give almost anything to be able to go back and do differently, but all we can do is ask for forgiveness and allow God to heal our broken hearts.

You are seen and you are loved. You are not evil and you are not worthless. God still has great plans for you. I encourage you to turn your mess into your message; use your story to help others. I pray for you the promises of Isaiah 61:3, that God would give you "a crown of beauty instead of ashes, the oil of joy instead of mourning, and a garment of praise instead of a spirit of despair."

CHAPTER TEN
Transitions

I walked across UCA's stage with a belly ready to pop and claimed my Bachelor of Arts degree two days before Ava was born. She was a perfect, beautiful baby girl, and I grieved when she was no longer just mine. I did not expect to feel so scared about having her, my heart, out in the big, bad world. I was eager to be an official family and share the same last name, so I was overjoyed that we had our wedding planned for two months later. My mom questioned whether I would regret packing so many major life milestones into such a short window of time, but I had given up the luxury of planning my life around my timeline; I hadn't been very good at it up until now anyway, I was just grateful for the amazing things happening in my life. Our relationship still struggled, but the night before I was to marry Matt, I got down on my knees and invited the Lord to shut the door if it was not His will. He did not shut the door; He gave me visions of the man Matt would become, of the couple we would become together, and I felt peace.

Ava was only two weeks old when I went to work full-time for a local newspaper. It was up the street from our condo. I would come home at lunch, breastfeed her, and cry when I had to leave. I would continue to leave her every day for a few more months while Matt stayed home with her. He would go out with his friends when I got home from work. Not great for a new marriage, but I didn't care. I just wanted time with Ava, and he needed to get out of the house. Eventually, we decided Matt would get a job and I would stay home with her. He did not have his degree, so he ended up managing a restaurant and kept horrible hours.

I loved spending every minute of every day with Ava. I worked out while she napped. I cooked, I cleaned, I read, and I rested. We went for lots of walks, went to parks, and would lie on a blanket in the yard and play with toys. I loved everything about being a stay-at-home mom. It's one of those seasons in life I am able to look back on and see the sweet provision of rest and quality time the Lord provided.

However, our marriage struggled. By one year in, I felt we had made a huge mistake, and I wasn't sure we would make it. Matt and I spent little, if any, quality time together. We carried financial stress, he was exhausted, and our communication skills had not improved past our dysfunctional loudness and anger from him and shutting down from me. To top it off, I did not trust the friends Matt spent time with (or Matt, if I am being honest), for good reason. So, I felt I needed to focus on my next move to make sure I would be able to provide all Ava needed on my own. I told him we would be moving with or without him to Tennessee. I don't know if that was the right thing to do, but I can say that at the time, I felt it was the only option.

Matt, Ava, and I moved from Arkansas to Tennessee when Ava was about two, and we were twenty-five, to be closer to my family. I wanted to go back to school, and they could help with childcare. When I would start to think I had gotten it all wrong and I wasn't meant to do more, the Lord would remind me about the Vanderbilt sign I saw at my last Rockette's practice. I thought Vanderbilt was probably out of my reach, but with the support of my family, I knew I could go back to school somewhere. The move itself was stressful enough, but when we arrived in Tennessee, Matt also found out the job he had lined up fell through. He wasn't as excited about the move as I was since his family and friends were in Arkansas, and now he didn't have a job. He was angry and depressed, and I was even more hopeless for us.

The heightened emotions and months of being stuck in fight-or-flight resulted in me having a flare. Matt convinced me to go to the ER, knowing that a steroid dose pack had provided relief in the past. I am glad I did, and this is a flare I remember because the doctor looked at me and said, "Don't take steroids anymore or you'll end up with diabetes." I don't know who that doctor was, but he was a Godsend because he was not wrong. This was the first time I truly trusted a doctor; it was also when I decided I couldn't trust our medical system. I realized the treatments being recommended for me would just cause other issues in the long term.

I was five years into the erythema nodosum diagnosis and had been absolutely tossed around and cast aside. This is when the lion inside of me started roaring. I was no longer a child—I was an adult, I was a mom, I was smart, I was sick, and I had a life worth living. I wanted answers. No one was rescuing me. I needed to advocate for myself. I started doing research and would bring articles to my PCP, who laughed at me, literally, as if I couldn't possibly know what I was talking about, but it wouldn't stop me.

After a few months, Matt and I were a bit steadier, and there was less day-to-day tension. I got a job as a chiropractic assistant, and Matt got a job waiting tables. I started asking God, "Okay, what's next? This can't be all there is for us." Then one day in 2004, a woman named Vicky, who is a friend and mentor of mine to this day, called me from Vanderbilt Peabody's School of Education. She let me know she had received my request for more information about the Child Studies Program and that she wanted to schedule a meeting and an interview. I had not requested information about the program; I had never even heard of it (*Hello, Lord!*). But now that I had, I wanted in.

We met for an interview, and it sounded incredible. It was basically a master's program studying child development, with courses and internships tailored to each student's interests. I was warned not to take the Graduate Record Examination without studying, but I was working doubles as a server at Mellow Mushroom when I wasn't working as the office manager and assistant at the chiropractic office. We were trying to save up money for a down payment on our first home. So, not having time or brain space to study, I took the exam against the warning, and I did not get the score Vanderbilt required. This was humbling, but I did not feel that it was God closing the door, just saying, "Not yet." So, I studied, and the next time there was a test window, I took it again and earned the score I needed.

That summer, we purchased a brand new home in a sweet subdivision about fifteen minutes from my parents, and that fall, I entered the child studies program. My mom helped with Ava while I went to school. I left the chiropractic job and picked up more shifts waiting tables. Matt was not having success finding meaningful or fruitful work, which caused more strain in our marriage and was not good for his battle with shame and feeling lost. The extra stress affected my health, but I did what I had learned to do: I put my head down and powered through because I didn't see another option.

Also about this time, at the age of twenty-six, I found a dermatologist online who seemed to know about erythema nodosum and was at Vanderbilt. I was at the tail end of a flare, so I scheduled an appointment with him as quickly as possible. He biopsied one of the nodules and gave me the diagnosis of "nodular vasculitis" instead of erythema nodosum. This meant I was having inflammation in the blood vessels, but we still didn't know the cause. I knew inflammation in my blood vessels couldn't be good, especially as often as it was happening.

I stood in his office with Matt and our toddler as I looked at him and asked him if it would kill me. I don't know what he was thinking, but the long pause and look of discomfort on his face before he answered with a very hesitant "no" did not give me much confidence. There was no digging deeper to determine what was causing the flares of vasculitis or treatment options other than those that weren't proven to be successful and carried their own risks. However, information was information, and I was cautiously optimistic with a diagnosis and a prognosis that, though unclear, tended slightly toward the positive. I carried on and dealt with flares as they came. I mostly tried to ignore them and surrender any fear that came with them to the Lord.

I had been researching the effect of chronic stress on the

body because I at least knew that played a role. I continued exercising, started practicing deep breathing, processed my emotions, and did my best to keep myself from going to the stress place in my mind. I worked on my communication and patience with Matt. I focused on my sleep and started eating organic food. I only took anti-inflammatories when the pain in my legs demanded attention, but otherwise, I was on no medication. I wanted to take a holistic and natural approach to being well. I knew God made my body to heal; I just needed to follow His lead to get there.

I don't know about you, but the verse "Come to me, all you who are weary and burdened, and I will give you rest " (Matthew 11:28), was one that always resonated with me. I always felt like I was weary and burdened. I was constantly striving to heal myself, to heal my marriage, and to create a healthy home, all while trying to make an income and make a way. Oh, how I wish I had learned what I now know way back then. Rest is such a gift, and sitting and waiting for the Lord's direction will save years—if not decades—of struggle and heartache.

Stress is a huge factor in all illnesses because it affects your hormones, inflammation, and immune function. Through my training and own experiences, I have a keen understanding of the interplay of stress and our emotional, spiritual, and physical well-being. And guess what? Resting is still something I have the hardest time doing. It is what I have to pray for the most. A great book to read if you want to learn more about the role of stress in your health as well as tools to manage stress is Dr. Don Colber's *Stress Less*.

I don't recommend becoming stressed about your stress. Instead, I encourage you to be teachable and ask the Lord to help you create habits that force you to be still and rest, like meditation, turning off all screens (especially your phone), and going for a walk in nature. Now, take a deep breath in over five seconds, hold it for five seconds, and blow it out over five seconds. Do that ten more times and you have a good tool to get you started in regulating your nervous system out of fight, flight, or freeze—stress mode.

CHAPTER ELEVEN
My Love Story is Not My Whole Story

I loved being a mama. Ava, about two-and-a-half at the time, started taking dance classes and was full of joy and determination. We played and painted together. We even came up with short stories; I chased her through the playground as she spouted out the details of the characters and events. I was in awe of her imagination. I could also study her as I studied child development. In my classes, I learned more about how traumatic home dysfunction could affect kids and was even more careful and intent on trying to keep the peace to protect her.

This usually meant I stuffed my feelings and did my best to manage Matt's so we could have a peaceful home. This, of course, wasn't great for my health or our relationship. Matt needed to feel and heal from whatever was keeping him angry. He didn't need to be managed; he needed to learn how to manage his own emotions. To do that, or even to be called up to that, he needed to be seen. I needed to feel safe and loved. Busyness and stress kept us from being what the other needed.

We had a great church, and I was active in the women's

ministry. I had encouraging people around me and a plan for my future that I was excited about, but I couldn't see how it would include Matt. We were living parallel lives, and when we did intersect, it usually wasn't positive. This is where I wish I could go back and get in Matt's face and ask him what he really wanted. I wish I had picked my head up and stopped powering through long enough to see he was suffering and to identify and face my pain as well. We were in a cycle of dysfunction and were missing one another.

I said I trusted the Lord and believed I did, but the cares of the world distracted me from waiting on Him and His plans. I felt pressure to hurry up and figure out a way to provide for us. The reality is that I didn't lift my eyes to notice what Matt needed, and he never took my face in his hands to see me either. I was doing what I thought I was supposed to do in order to take care of Ava and me, as I gave up hope or any expectation of a healthy marriage. I felt like an all-around failure. I felt like life was spinning around me and all I could do was say, "Jesus, help."

One day, while I was journaling and praying to the Lord, I told him, "I give. Have your way." I heard Him say "Your love story is not your whole story." He was faithful and would allow for other parts of my story to expand and carry me when my love story couldn't. My love story was, in fact, not my whole story, but it affected every other part of my story, and it would demand attention from time to time. God was clearly working in the other areas; school and Ava became my focus.

Remember how God told me that I would help lots of other young women like me when I was walking the eating disorder journey? Well, in the child studies program, I was able to study eating disorders, their causes, and their treatments. I did an internship with Vanderbilt's Pediatric Eating Disorder Clinic, and—get this—the Medical Director was trained by Dr. Portilla, my doctor from Arkansas (God is so cool, yes?!). I also completed a research internship with their Psychology Department. They were studying the association between anxiety and chronic stomach pain in kids. I also worked as a research assistant for a professor at Vanderbilt, which paid for my tuition. This was incredible! God was all over this. I loved every minute of it and was sure I was finally on the path God had for me.

During graduation season, the question was *okay, now what?* I could either pursue a PhD in psychology or I could apply for Vanderbilt's Nurse Practitioner Bridge program where I could enter with any degree (yes, even my writing degree), become a registered nurse in three semesters, and become a nurse practitioner in three more. It would be an incredibly intense and stressful undertaking, but I would graduate with a Master of Science in Nursing degree and could specialize in psychiatry, which would make me a valuable member of an eating disorder treatment team. I decided this was the route I wanted to take, and after an incredible interview with the head of the Psychiatric Nurse Practitioner Program, I was accepted.

Right about this time, my marriage took a nosedive, and my love story was demanding attention. Now about four years in, Matt seemed more and more unhappy; drinking, an old coping mechanism, made a comeback, and he was more emotionally and physically disengaged and checked out. Maybe it was because I was finding my path forward and he felt like he was stuck. My old coping mechanisms of putting walls up to protect, believing I was better off alone, also reared back up.

We lacked connection and unity, which we both desired. Resentment was growing in our marriage, and tensions were high in our home. It was a dark season for us. One day at church, with nothing to offer for a tithe (literally, we had no money), I took a ring off my finger that Matt had given me for an anniversary, dropped it in the offering basket, and told the Lord I was giving Him my marriage and that I needed clarity. Within a few days, I felt I had clarity about Matt and me being on different paths. I was building a future and wanted a healthy home for Ava and myself. Matt didn't seem to want the same things. I didn't feel supported or loved, and I was tired; we were no good together. We needed to set each other free. I told him I wanted a divorce.

This is when the betrayal came to light for me. He confessed about the other relationship he was in before we got married. He said he felt he needed to confess so that our marriage had a chance to be healthy. I, however, felt strongly that he should've confessed *before* asking me to marry him. I know it's crazy, but from my perspective, even though our relationship was not healthy when we were dating, I never thought he was capable of cheating. It was one of the reasons I kept going back to him and staying when other parts of our relationship weren't good.

I had existing wounds from men not being faithful and sexualizing women. Throughout my life, I truly wondered if men of integrity actually existed. But Matt seemed different. He was someone who would look away when lingerie commercials would come on TV without me ever saying anything to him about it. As far as I knew, he wasn't partaking in porn, and as far as I knew, the two years we dated, albeit on and off, he never dated or had relations with anyone else. I saw him as safe in that respect. I was learning that I knew very little about who he really was or what really happened.

The moments that followed his confession are a blur of swirling emotions and words. I was obliterated from the inside out. I had been completely played and manipulated. I felt so many things in a matter of seconds, but what stuck was that *I was cheated*. Not just "cheated on," but *cheated*. I felt like he had tricked me into marrying him. He was instantly a stranger to me. As much as I did not feel content with the man I had just told I wanted to divorce, I realized in this moment that I needed that guy. The irony was not lost on me; the man who hurt me was the man I needed to comfort me, but he didn't exist anymore. Similar to when my eating disorder friend in high school deceived and abandoned me, I was left to face this alone.

I quickly texted my mom to pick up Ava so that I could say what I really needed to say aloud. I refused to talk anymore about it until Ava was gone, but it didn't stop him from desperately following me around the house and asking me to talk. I didn't want to talk. I wasn't crying; I was in shock. I was planning my life without him quickly. I wanted him to disappear forever. I emailed our realtor and asked her to list our house. If I knew the steps to a quick divorce and if I could put thoughts together other than thinking I would ruin Ava if we did divorce, I would've filed that day. My confidence was destroyed. Not only could I not trust him, I could no longer trust myself. *How did I miss this?*

Confessing his betrayal years after the fact made me question every day that we spent together and every memory we had made since that betrayal. He and this girl had secrets from me—secrets they shared that I felt kept them close and drove me further away. Spinning in my thoughts and emotions, I was afire with anger. I wondered who else knew, was in on it, and was lying to me as well. *Did my "friends" help him betray me? Did they know when they watched me walk down the aisle, committing to a life with him? Was he still in contact with her?* There were so many questions, and even though he said it meant nothing to him and he wished he could go back and do everything differently, none of the answers he gave satisfied me. There was no justifying something that was unjustifiable; there was no putting my heart back together or easing my pain. My love story had been hijacked and was veering off course. I would have to walk the path out one day at a time.

If you are walking through betrayal, I am praying for you right now. I pray that you allow God to hold space for you to process your emotions safely and that you surrender your heart, your pain, and your love story to Him. It is through your surrender that He is able to show Himself faithful as He meets you and continues to reveal His good plans for you. Take a deep breath in and surrender. You are seen, you are loved, and you deserve to be protected.

I wish I had, again, been still and rested with the Lord before I responded and reacted. A verse that I wish I had focused on during this time is James 1:19 that encourages us to be "quick to listen, slow to speak and slow to become angry." It was not the wisdom I enacted during this event, but it is something I have prayed for over the years in our marriage. If we can just take a pause, breathe, pray, and respond from a place of wisdom and understanding instead of fear, pain, and blind rage, the outcome is one hundred percent likely to be more positive.

CHAPTER TWELVE
The Aftermath of Betrayal

In the wake of the confession, I got sick a few weeks later with one of the worst flares to date. Having just graduated from the master of education program, I was preparing to start the nurse practitioner program, which had been called "one of the most rigorous and challenging things I would ever do" by the professors at the school of nursing. During this time, I only had the strength and emotional willpower to ignore Matt. I could not engage in any fights while I lay in bed with a fever of 105 degrees. He expected me to hear his confession and release him from his shame, as if I had the power to do that. That was something he would need to work out with the Lord within himself.

He wanted me to "get over" his betrayal quickly. Just like with the eating disorder, I wished it could be that easy. I was bombarded by intruding thoughts. I replayed the "what ifs" over and over in my head. I wanted to go back in time and do everything after I found out I was pregnant differently. I wanted to be alone with the Lord and Ava. I felt stuck in the marriage and stuck in an unhealthy body. I was hopeless.

Matt also felt helpless and scared. He wanted to take me

to the emergency department. I knew by now they wouldn't know what to do with me. I had learned to ride the flares out and trust the Lord, whether that was right or wrong. It was the only option I had, and Jesus was always enough. I was also angry with Matt and felt he didn't have any right to act like he cared; I didn't even want to see him. I felt sure he and our marriage would be the literal death of me.

I closed my eyes and surrendered to the Lord, begging Him to heal me or take me.

"I am protecting your organs," He whispered immediately. I won't lie, I thought, *Okay... Thank you, but I don't fully understand.* I was hoping the fever would lift and the headache and body pain would go away in one miraculous moment. Now, equipped with medical knowledge, I do understand. Terrifying things can happen to you with high fevers and chronic systemic inflammation. I am grateful that He was protecting my organs, and I am grateful that His Word never changes, because every time I had a flare thereafter, I would remind my body, spirit, soul, and the enemy that God was protecting my organs. He was faithful and was already in my future, calling out to me, protecting me, and encouraging me.

As I was reeling and trying to re-stabilize, life did not stop or even slow down. It doesn't unless we force it to, and that often doesn't seem like an option. I wish I had sat down in the wilderness and told the Lord to take over. I wish I had rested and healed. I did not. We had no money and, now, no relationship; all I had was a daughter who depended on me and a path forward. I felt I had to carry on as a mom and student. I didn't file for divorce. I didn't have the energy to figure out what all it entailed or the money for a lawyer. My mind was numb. I was just existing, and when I could think, I played out imaginary scenarios for how the secret relationship happened over and over.

Matt started going to counseling. When we went to our church counselor after the confession, he was concerned about the shame that Matt carried. I agreed because I knew if someone didn't face their shame and release it, they would inevitably feel worse about themselves and would continue to project and act out in their relationships. I'd had enough of that. I also had wounds that would need tending to. I couldn't stay guarded in the marriage—I would have to get to a place where I felt safe and could be vulnerable.

I was hopeful that counseling might help Matt, that he could become a true spiritual leader in our home, and that we might have a shot at a healthy marriage. I will say to all churches that couples turn to in times of crisis such as this: you need to put more energy into the victim of betrayal, no matter how strong she seems. After all, I was the one battling and questioning everything in my life. I was the one who no longer had a firm foundation upon which to stand. I was sinking, and I was in a war that no one could see. Matt had taken the enemy off his back and thrown him onto mine, *literally*.

The healing in our relationship and in my heart could have come faster, and the journey could've been less traumatic and complicated if, after he confessed, I saw the fruit of repentance and a heart change in him. I didn't. Nothing was healthier in our home. He was defensive, and his counselor was not someone I would call life-giving or effective. If anything, he created more confusion and division. This serves as a reminder to be very prayerful and to do your due diligence before letting any counselor speak into your life.

Pray for discernment as you are taking counsel; not all of it is right for you.

I know some of you are walking through similar circumstances. There is no shame in what you are feeling. Anger is justified. I will warn you, whatever you do, do *not* watch *Sliding Doors* with Gwyneth Paltrow. It will only enrage you more. I would encourage you to choose to forgive as quickly as possible. *Wait!* Let me explain. In choosing forgiveness, you are aligning yourself with the will of God and hedging yourself in protection from anger taking hold of you for good. Righteous anger is justified, but anger-turned-resentment will distract you from your faith, hope, security, and identity in the Lord and what He is doing in your story.

Pray that your heart stays soft in order to hear God's voice. Feelings of forgiveness will not follow right away, but by choosing to forgive and submit the situation to the Lord, you are protecting yourself from the enemy and hedging yourself in God's love and peace. You are not condoning what was done to you; you are releasing the person who did it to the Lord. You will have to do it daily, and often multiple times a day, until you don't have to anymore because peace has come.

Ask the questions you need answers to, but know that there is no answer that will make it make sense or make you feel any better. Forgiveness does not always mean reconciliation either. We can't force another to surrender their heart to the Lord and truly be repentant. Tuck into the Lord as deep as you can and see your situation from a heavenly perspective. Imagine yourself sitting next to Jesus in Heaven and looking down on the situation... it's much clearer from a higher vantage point and from a place of safety with Jesus.

As Romans 12:2 reminds us that we should "not conform

to the pattern of this world, but be transformed by the renewing of [our] minds." Ask God to fill you with peace, shower you with love, permeate you with patience, and saturate you with joy. Walk slowly, take your time, and give yourself time to regain your footing before you make decisions. My story will not be everyone's story, nor should it. Reach out to someone you know you can process with and get support from, who will not speak ill of your marriage or spouse but will constantly point you back to the Lord and will seek His will with you (hint: this is most likely not going to be family, as they have a hard time not being biased). Also, be careful who you share with. I had friends I reached out to who said, "It was four years ago; why does it matter?" I felt like they were saying, "Get over it. Even though you were betrayed, broken to your core, and feel like you don't even know the man you married, your emotions have no merit." I quickly realized that some people could be shared with and others would need to be avoided during this time.

CHAPTER THIRTEEN
Spiritual Warfare

With another school semester starting and life's demands continuing, I did not take time to properly process my emotions and brokenness in the marriage. I sought and went to counseling; I did, but this wound went deep. I needed more intensive help than a counselor looking at me and saying, "He didn't have feelings for her; it was really no different from masturbation." Thanks, lady, but that doesn't help; I would not appreciate my husband doing either (again, be careful who you allow to counsel you and speak into your life and marriage). We sold our home and bought a condo closer to Vanderbilt. I started school and was one of only a few "older" students who were moms with young kids (in reality, I was only twenty-eight).

I remember getting into fights on the phone with Matt just before I would walk in to take exams because, of course, we had not had a great morning before I left for school. I'm sure it wasn't true, but it sometimes felt like he wanted me to fail. I did the only thing I could do: I worked harder. The already sky-high walls between us got thicker. He was angry that he wasn't getting the response from me that he wanted.

I think the enemy had convinced him that after he confessed, everything would be rainbows and butterflies—that I would be grateful for his honesty and all would be well in our relationship. His pressuring me to hurry up and get over it inevitably pushed me further away.

Knowing what I know now, I am quite sure that I spent much of this year completely dissociated, a survival skill I developed from childhood trauma. On top of everything else, we did not have a dependable income, so we were financially stressed, too. The only way I made it through this time was by knowing there was hope; there was a light at the end of the financial tunnel. But I felt the pressure because I also knew I was the only one who could get us there. It would be three years of hell physically, mentally, and emotionally, but I was determined to do this for Ava. I would deal with our marriage later.

We moved into a condo, and Ava loved it. She made friends quickly with the other children, as well as with the older single women who lived in the condos next to ours. I was halfway through the NP program, and now a registered nurse. We started our clinical training for the psychiatric specialty, which meant we were going into psychiatric hospitals and inpatient facilities. Because of the constant stress and unresolved emotions, I had back-to-back flares, which meant chronic systemic inflammation and dysfunction. I found myself again in a chronic state of fight-or-flight. My adrenals were shot. I did not know what was happening in my body at the time. I could not think clearly, and I was having out-of-body experiences daily, sometimes multiple times a day.

In addition to the physical symptoms, I was clearly under spiritual attack. The spirit of anxiety that was broken off of me when I was a teenager was back, and he brought friends. I wasn't strong enough to take him this time. I didn't know what to do. We had already reached out to the church's pastoral counselor and sought counselors on our own. It seemed that no one could see that I needed deliverance. I was fragile, and I was barely making it.

I truly believed that if I felt anything or had any emotion, I would break; that my brain would shatter and I would never recover. I didn't want Ava's story to include a mom who went to a psych hospital for a nervous breakdown, even though I was sure I was having one. I resolved to stay emotionally flat, not allowing myself to feel or react to anything. I still had hurt—sadness, confusion, and anger toward Matt raging through every part of my body—but I shut it all down so the stress of it would not kill me, and I made the decision every day to forgive him.

One night as I lay in bed, I felt the Lord wanted me to tell Matt I *truly* forgave him. This was for me more than him. I had told him before but we still felt distant, and now, it was coming from a place of surrender, not just a choice I was making while battling anger. I was ready to lay anger down to replace it with peace. I did not want to be alone. I needed Matt to be my husband. I needed him to walk with me. It was time for the feelings to follow my decision to forgive.

So, in an attempt to salvage what we could of our relationship and hopefully build upon it into a healthier one, I told him I forgave him. I was not prepared for his response, which was, "Good, because I can't keep living like this." What I heard was that he was saying he would leave if I wasn't able to get over it. That if I could not wrestle the devil off my back, the one he threw at me from his own, he would leave me so he wouldn't have to watch anymore or experience the consequences. As he said those words, I felt not only betrayed but rejected and completely abandoned.

What I needed was for him to pray with me, tell me everything would be okay, and hold me. He did not yet have the emotional or spiritual maturity to respond in that way, and the way I had been acting did not invite the response I was needing. He couldn't have had any idea how his words of disregard would unhinge any tempering I was able to do with the emotions inside of me. I was forced to feel things I had been shutting down. I felt the tremendous fear that had been hiding behind the anger. I felt all of the existing wounds from childhood that this new trauma was poking at. I tried to become numb again, but the enemy was already in my head, and he had a new message. He told me Matt and Ava would be better off without me.

One day soon after that night, the enemy went on to tell me that stress wouldn't kill me but that I would in fact do it myself, and he would make sure of it. I'll never forget it. We went to my least favorite psych facility for clinicals for the nursing program. It was a heartbreaking and frightening place, and I did not feel or see Jesus there—just darkness and hopelessness. We watched a video on schizophrenia and how it typically emerges under extreme stress before the age of thirty. I was under extreme stress and just so happened to be twenty-nine; I had never wanted to be older more than I did that day.

Following the video, we went to do an exercise with the patients, which was to play music, take them from their chairs, and ask them to dance. I went to a slim, tender looking woman staring down at her shoes, probably in her early sixties. She looked up at me and gave me a half-hearted smile.

"I can't dance," she said before slowly revealing her bandaged wrists as tears welled up in her eyes. "I don't even remember it. My mind just snapped, and they said I tried to kill myself."

Fear rose in me like a tidal wave as the enemy told me, "That is what will happen to you." I now believed I couldn't even trust myself for protection.

I pulled my professor aside and told her I was anxious and needed to leave. She looked at me and said, "Karen, anxiety is a spirit, and you need to tell it to go, in Jesus' name." I don't know how the university would have felt about her expressing her spiritual beliefs, but I am grateful beyond words for her boldness. She somehow knew I was a sister in Christ and what I was really battling. I think she knew this spirit personally and had victory over it in her own life. I knew from my past battles with anxiety how to identify the enemy and his lies, but now I knew how to bind him up and cast him out— how to neutralize him.

Armed with new tactics and a fresh battle cry, I started speaking out loud whenever I felt overcome with anxiety, which was often. I told the spirit to go in Jesus' name. I'm sure many women in the bathroom stalls next to me either thought I was losing it or benefited from the warfare in the next stall. I don't know, but I didn't care. This was life or death, and I wasn't going down easy. Did it work? Yes. Every time, I had peace afterward. Did it last? Sometimes longer than others, but I remained consistent, reminding my spirit and the enemy, who was really in control and to whom I belonged. Sometimes it felt like I cast the spirit of anxiety down hundreds of times a day.

I battled where I could and surrendered the battling I could not do to the Lord. I spent less time stressing about school and more time in the Word. Ava used to say, "Mom's doing her God time," because that is what I would do as soon as I got home from school. I had various translations of the Bible and would sit on my bedroom floor pouring over them all; the book of Job resonated with me during this season. He knew and was an example of what I was walking through, and his story highlighted God's faithfulness. If God could deliver Job, I knew He could deliver me, too. Job's story was what I needed, and I can't wait to hug his neck when I get to Heaven. The anxiety became less and less debilitating, but pursuing the Lord as hard and often as I was, I still felt far from Him and would find myself on my face in sobs, just begging Him to come close.

One night, I had a dream that I was casting out demons. Hand outstretched, no fear, using my new weapon of warfare, binding and casting. When I woke, I felt something leave the room. My hands were clasped tightly together, as if I had been praying in my sleep, and my fingers were numb. I had a few more exorcism dreams after that and joked with the Lord that I had asked for gifts of the spirit, but did exorcism have to be the one He gave me first?

During this time and the previous few months, I had eliminated all distractions in my pursuit of the Lord and His peace; all I listened to was worship music, and I did not watch TV. I didn't like it at first, I won't lie. I couldn't stand some of the songs, but I decided I was going to fake it until I made it, just like eating and teaching my body to feel hungry again. I would learn to like it. It was powerful to remain in a posture of praise while I battled, and it is something I carried with me from this experience. It reminded my spirit that God was in control and that He was still with me, even when I didn't feel Him.

I truly believe something powerful happened in the spiritual realm the night I encountered and cast away demons. For the days following, darkness continued to lift. I recognized my reflection in the mirror. I wasn't scared to be left alone with knives in the house or even my razor in the shower. The spirit of anxiety, like any other bully, got bored and left me alone. This time, it broke off of me for good. I have never had to battle that debilitating spirit of anxiety again, even as I have gone through more trials. If I think I catch even a glimpse of it, you better believe I know to cast it down immediately.

A book that helped me during this time–not a Christian book, but it made me feel less "crazy" and normalized the feelings I was having while empowering me to continue to walk forward—was *From Panic to Power* by Lucinda Bassett. I highly recommend it if you or someone you know is dealing with anxiety. If you are battling thoughts of suicide, please reach out to someone you trust or even a suicide hotline (you can call or text 988). Because I know you are knit together as a complex being of body-spirit-soul, I also recommend you seek counseling, and consult a functional medicine provider who can help you get to the root of any issues with hormones, nutrients, chronic infections, and lifestyle habits to better support you as you heal from trauma. Having good, godly people in your life to pray for and encourage you is also important.

Surrender your heart to the Lord in your battle. Put on your spiritual armor and cast the enemy down. Remember, "For our struggle is not against flesh and blood, but against the rulers, against the authorities, against the powers of this dark world and against the spiritual forces of evil in the heavenly realms" (Ephesians 6:12). The first step to being successful in battle is correctly identifying your enemy. Remove distractions and turn your eyes toward the Lord as you worship. Fake it until you make it if you have to, but no matter what, as long as you don't give up and you keep pursuing and inviting the Lord in, you will make it; God will change your heart.

Like Job's story was for me, I hope my story is one that encourages you in your pit. He was faithful to meet me and lead me out, and He will be faithful to you as well.

CHAPTER FOURTEEN
Two Hearts Redeemed

Moving into the last year of the NP program, we were in the aftermath of the storm in our marriage, and I was in the aftermath of the storm in my body, spirit, and soul. I wanted to quit school; if working as an RN was an option, I would have. But I was in a "bridge program," and we weren't earning a BSN, so we had to go all of the way through to get our MSN if we planned to become licensed practitioners. Since I couldn't quit, the next best thing was to switch specialties. As much as I wanted to work with people who were suffering with life and all of its challenges, I needed out of the psychiatric specialty. I needed to keep chasing the peace I had recently found, and it would not be in psychiatric facilities.

I changed my program to women's health. It was the only specialty program with openings, but it was a blessing; just what I needed. I was surrounded by women, mostly coming in for well visits and pregnancy checks. The environment was fun, joy-filled, and peaceful. I had a clinical preceptor who was kind and encouraging. My adrenals had some time to calm. I was healing, feeling emotionally stable, and having fewer flares. I continued to forgive Matt daily. The enemy had no new tricks, so as he kept trying to regain control by triggering me with thoughts that had the potential to stir anger, I remained on guard.

Matt and I had moments of light in the darkness. I was hopeful that we were healing. We even started talking about trying for another baby. During one of the moments of light, when our walls came down and we connected emotionally and physically, God did bless us with new life. Ava had popped into my bathroom when she was about three years old while I was getting ready for work one morning. "Mom, I prayed for a baby brother," she announced. Well, she got that baby brother, Tyler, in the spring of her fifth year. Just like Ava, he has been nothing short of a miracle, an incredible blessing, and a source of joy since day one.

When Tyler was born I was completing my clinicals for school. Though I wasn't working a full-time job, it was just as, if not a more stressful time. I had homework, exams, and was preparing to sit for the National Council Licensure Examination (NCLEX) and the Nursing Boards. I was also starting to think about jobs after school. With my whole heart, I just wanted to stay home with my babies, but I was the one with the education and, now, a lot of student loan debt. I was trapped—forever. It felt incredibly hopeless. I started having frequent flares again and pressed harder into the Lord for help with my physical health.

One morning, while watching *Joyce Meyer Ministries*, which was a mainstay in my life, Dr. Colbert was on as a guest. He was a functional medicine doctor in Florida that Joyce had used to guide her own wellness journey, and he was talking about a "biblical" approach to healing. I ordered his book, *Bible Cure for Autoimmune Disorders*. Matt and I prioritized buying more expensive organic food and having less processed food in our home so that I could follow the diet recommendations. I added the suggested dietary supplements, prayed the specific prayers for healing, and implemented the stress reduction techniques. My body became more balanced, and I felt empowered to play an active role in my health.

My physical health was more stable, and I felt I could safely explore my emotions and start doing heart-healing work. I know this will shock you, but adding the stress of another innocent child depending on you to stay alive did not help our already fragile relationship. Between finishing school, my physical health, finances, a new baby, and our own unhealthy coping mechanisms, Matt and I didn't feel more connected; we felt worlds apart. I was at a loss for how to even begin the healing of our marriage. I had a very real conversation with Matt one day where I let him know that I would always love him, but I could not stay in a loveless and angry marriage. I had witnessed them and always thought, *What is the point? I would rather be single and lonely than married and lonely, walking on eggshells in my own home.* We would need to lay down all resentment, forgive one another —truly forgive—and let the past stay covered by the blood of Jesus. We locked eyes that day and committed to locking arms moving forward in the battle for our marriage and family.

It was not going to be easy, but I knew what I needed to do, and that was the opposite of everything I had tried in the past. I needed to truly release our marriage to the Lord, love

Matt right where he was, as he was, and stay focused on my own growth and heart healing. I remained hopeful. The good news is that God was able to work in our hearts since we laid down our anger and resentment and were inviting Him in to heal us and our marriage, as a couple. I used my words instead of putting up walls and pushing Matt away. I asked forgiveness when I acted or reacted in a way that created division, and was quick to forgive when he apologized. I was starting to see the fruit of what God was doing in Matt as he was opening his heart and spirit to the Lord. He became gentler in his responses to me and his reprimands to the kids. As I felt safer, my defenses were less and less. I also realized I was starting to truly like my husband, which, in turn, illuminated that I hadn't for a lot of our marriage up until this point. I had resentment, disappointment, and bitterness toward him that blocked me from wanting to know him in order to love him better. I can't speak for him, but I would venture to say he felt the same, and as we were each moving closer to the Lord individually, it allowed us to also move closer to one another.

For our marriage to become a love story of thriving instead of striving, Matt and I both needed our hearts changed; we needed to learn to see one another through God's eyes consistently, not just every once in a while when we were having a good day and chose to. Ultimately, we would need to end our marriage as it was and allow God to create a new one. We knew we couldn't change ourselves, only God could do that as we continually chose to do better. We consistently prayed together, out loud, with one another and our children. Where repentance and forgiveness were needed, they were granted. When we forgave, it didn't mean we forgot. Thoughts would come. Triggers would come. We would sometimes get so deep into fights that we would find ourselves worlds apart again. One of us would be brave enough to scale the walls around the other to say, "Hey, I don't even know how we got here. This isn't us anymore; we don't operate like this. I am sorry." We didn't need to beat each other over the head with what went wrong or why; our goal was unity, and we fought for it.

We would encounter bumps in the road, but the important thing was to get over them intact, and faster each time, as we kept moving forward in healing. It was none of my business what God was doing in my husband. It was my job to pray without ceasing. I was responsible for myself, my attitude, and my actions. I knew God could do the miracles needed for our marriage to survive and be healthy. He had healed me before, He had redeemed Job, and He could do this.

There were many days I had to lay the marriage down again when I realized I had picked it up and was trying to make it work myself. I wanted faster healing. I wanted love, safety, companionship, and for everything to *just be okay*. I tended to be the peacemaker in our relationship, but I needed to stop trying to fix things. The Lord was teaching me to trust Him and that He would take care of me and our children. He often gave me the vision of the husband He created Matt to be, the same one He gave me the night before our wedding. I needed that man. I knew that was who Matt was becoming, and I had to get out of God's way.

Over time, as the waves of pain and healing would come, the Lord accomplished a great work in my heart. He transformed my ability to grasp the truth that my identity, value, and worth were found solely in Him, not in how my husband or anyone else saw me or treated me. I no longer had insecure attachment within my marriage, and that is what enabled me to truly release it. That is when I started to have the clarity that would allow me to find the path to restoration for us. In my new confidence, I sought to understand my husband and what he needed instead of pointing my finger at him for not giving me what I needed.

I saw clearly that Matt's actions and choices that caused me pain were not a reflection of his love for me but instead of his own pain and brokenness. I had to see past anger and rise above the pride and fleshly desire to return hurt for the hurt and to enter into whatever was causing his pain, battling for him there. He was not my enemy. Nothing will change a marriage for the better quite like taking up the sword for your spouse against the true enemy; God can do powerful work in that unity and covenantal commitment. My personal healing ultimately allowed me to release Matt from any expectation I had of him filling gaps that only the Lord could fill in me. As Matt healed, he released me, too. This took the pressure off our relationship, and we both settled into feeling truly safe in our marriage for the first time ever, at about seventeen years in.

In what seemed like one day, because that is often how God works, the storms in our marriage halted. It was like the hand of God moved and the wind stopped blowing; tension was gone. We were able to stand without fighting for our balance. We were able to see clearly and feel the sunshine on our faces. I know that is not really how it happened because we both have many scars to say otherwise, but it is how it feels now looking back. All of the sudden, we had a breakthrough, and not a moment too late.

Today, I can wholeheartedly say that my heart belongs to the Lord, and I know I will be okay no matter what happens in my marriage, day-to-day or long-term. This allows me to find joy, peace, and comfort with Matt. God continues to heal what needs to be healed in our hearts and breaks off of us what needs to be broken. We have now been married for almost twenty-two years and have known one another for more than half of our lives. Do we do the healthy marriage thing perfectly? Ha! No. But we do our best, and we always strive to do even better, all while keeping Jesus at the center.

I truly like and love Matt, and I believe he truly likes and loves me. He is more and more the man God allowed me to see through His eyes almost twenty-two years ago. I grieve for the time we wasted pushing one another away. I am praying and believing that the years the enemy stole from us will be returned (Deuteronomy 30:3-13). There were so many! It breaks my heart and makes me mad to see how the enemy whipped us around for years in such a way that we couldn't even see straight. Our love story isn't one most would desire, but it is ours, and we are proud of our scrappy marriage; it is one of brokenness, God's faithfulness, healing, and redemption.

Maybe we would've had easier paths if we had divorced, but I am so grateful we didn't. I don't know if you have heard the saying "Wounds happen in relationships and wounds heal in relationships," but I believe that is true. I think marriage has the ability to be the rock tumbler and the healing balm that we need in different areas and seasons, to polish and heal us. The longer we are married and engage in the battles for one another's hearts, the sweeter the victories and the deeper our love can grow as we are safe places for one another to become more and more our authentic selves, the way God created us.

God knew we needed one another. Through our marriage, God has used us to become the people He created us to be. Matt is a spiritual leader and sounding board for me now. He is my prayer partner and an encouragement when I wrestle with doubt. Do old hurts come back up and threaten to steal our peace? At times. But we use communication to draw us closer when the circumstances threaten to create a divide. We strive to operate with ongoing humility, grace, and respect. We are committed to pursuing one another's hearts and to pointing one another back to the Lord. After all, hopelessness expands when our focus is on our flesh—on what the world and society would tell us to do. But we have found hope for our marriage and safety for our hearts in God's presence within us and at the center of our marriage. We have found that it is all we need.

Allowing God to heal our marriage is also healing wounds in the hearts of our children. They now witness love and respect in our home. They see that we truly like and love one another. Ava says she tells her friends that the couple they see now when they meet her parents is not the couple she grew up with as her parents. Both kids sometimes have a hard time believing the change is real and permanent, but trust is earned over time, and we have all the time in the world left. Trust is being rebuilt between all of us. We refuse to look back or go back to the old ways that were painful and unhealthy, like Lot's wife, who looked back and turned to a pillar of salt (Genesis 19:26). We pray that God continues to grow us closer to Him and one another daily, making us the man and woman, spouses, and parents He created us to be.

For those who have been through divorce, I am on my

knees for you today. There is no shame that you should hold. I don't know your story, and even if in your story you did something that ultimately played a role in the divorce, I hope you can see by now that you are not alone in being broken. I'm right there with you. The good news is that God sees you in your pain; He loves you, forgives you, and has healing and a good future for you and your family. After all, in Isaiah 61:1, Jesus says He came to bind up broken hearts. He wouldn't be sent to do that if God didn't already know His people would experience it. Plead the blood of Jesus and His living water over yourself, your situation, and your kids daily. He is faithful, and you are loved.

If you are separated or struggling in your marriage, I encourage you to reach out to mentors who are *for* marriage and who are for healthy relationships with healthy individuals in them. I encourage you to get counseling or coaching and face your own brokenness. Call everything from darkness into light and engage in the battle for your marriage and family. Put God in the middle of your relationship and your home. Put on your armor and go to battle for your spouse, not against. Remember: be slow to anger and slow to speak, for as Proverbs 15:18 says, "A hot tempered person stirs up conflict, but the one who is patient calms a quarrel."

You want to create peace so that God has the space to heal. I learned the Greek words *hupomone* (which means "steadfast," "constancy," and "endurance") and *macrothumia* (which means "true patience" and "long-suffering"). It is through long-suffering and enduring strength found by surrendering to the Lord that you will develop true patience and steadfast constancy, enabling you to withstand the storms and maintain your peace through trials (Romans 5:3). You will come out stronger on the other side, and I pray that your relationship will as well.

I encourage you to ask the Lord to change your heart toward your spouse and to allow you to see your spouse through His eyes. Then, double down and be willing to do the work. It's hard, so hard, and it can take time and suffering, but it is worth it.

CHAPTER FIFTEEN

Seeds Planted, a Life in Bloom

I felt compelled to work in functional medicine after I graduated from the NP program, so I poured over classified ads online. There were no such things as LinkedIn and Indeed—no easy job boards on the Internet through which to find jobs—but I found a functional medicine doctor, Dr. Michael Bernui, who was looking for a nurse practitioner. His office was about an hour's drive from our condo. By this time, Tyler was about eight months old, and Ava was six years old. It was heart-wrenching to leave my kids for so long every day, but I saw the value in what I was doing because I was learning what I knew would benefit not only myself and my family but so many others who were struggling like I was.

Dr. Bernui taught me functional medicine and how we needed to get to the root cause of symptoms and illnesses, then support the body in healing and detoxification. He taught me to see the patient as a whole, body, spirit, and soul, not as one organ system at a time as our medical model tends to do. He was also an example of a godly man and provider who was bold enough to share that he got up before the sun every morning to pray in his basement before his family woke. I also witnessed him praying with his patients, something I would incorporate into my practice moving forward. At this time, Matt had settled into a job with UPS and kept crazy and unpredictable hours. So, I eventually left the clinic job because I needed to be closer to home and my kids. I was heartbroken, but I knew God would keep using what I had learned in my practice moving forward, and that He would keep blessing Dr. Bernui's practice.

I went on to work in other functional medicine practices, with each doctor having a different skill set and focus. This allowed me to see the functional medicine approach done in different ways. It was incredible to help so many people and to continue to learn, but I often felt frustrated and defeated because through it all, I would still get flares despite the new interventions I now had knowledge of and access to. I remember times I would go to my hot car in the middle of summer to close my eyes for a few minutes in between patients because I couldn't get my fever down and was freezing. The exhaustion I would get with the flares I described as "comatose tired." I felt like I could fall into a deep sleep at any moment. I have never been a napper, so when I required a nap, I knew my body was struggling and I could expect a flare.

I covered my legs with pants or skirts and never mentioned anything to my patients. I figured if I was going to go down, I wanted to go down doing what I loved, and that was helping others. I also knew it was not God's plan to bring me as far as He had just to take me home before I could really fulfill my purpose. I would focus on my patients and power through, and when I finally got home, I would crash. Ibuprofen was the only thing that would touch the fevers and headaches, but there were times it didn't work, and I hated taking it because I knew it was not without its own risks.

During the peaks of the flares, I would wake up in the middle of the night with a bone-chilling cold that nothing would relieve except for a hot bath. I would psych myself up to get out from under the covers to draw a bath as I sat in tears on the cold ceramic, willing the water to come faster so I could be enveloped by warmth. Around 2014, I purchased an infrared dome that became my saving grace. I could lie in bed, turn it on, and put it over me. I was cocooned in heat.

I did not have an appetite while the flare was at its worst, either. I was not someone who would tell anyone how bad I was feeling or that I needed help. I also didn't have the energy to teach anyone how to care for me in those moments, so I would lie in bed and think of all of the things I knew my body needed and what I would do for someone else, but all I had was Jesus. I would remind Him that He said He was protecting my organs. Eventually, the fevers would break and I would start feeling better again.

As I mentioned in a previous chapter, I have always felt blessed because the flares from start to finish usually lasted about a month, but the worst part was high fevers that typically lasted only a few days to a week. When I wasn't having a flare, I was strong, healthy, and had no issues. With less stress from our marriage and being more financially stable, in addition to the functional medicine interventions, the flares were much less frequent by this time.

After about five years of working in other functional medicine practices, I opened my own and was able to create care plans and approach the wellness of my patients in my own way while drawing from all I had learned from the incredible doctors and mentors I had been blessed to work alongside. I loved the freedom of it and knowing it was mine and the Lord's. He continued to allow me to minister to many others. However, I was still raising kids and owning my own business as a one-woman show. From office manager to nurse practitioner and everything in between, it was a huge time commitment and a lot of pressure. Matt and I made the difficult decision, after about two years of owning my practice, to merge with another and let it go. We needed the security of a dependable income and needed to start saving. We also needed the time and brain space to continue to sow into one another and our children.

    I was offered a position as the Medical Director and Nurse Practitioner of the Hope Clinic for Women in Nashville, where God allowed me to be a part of an amazing team. I felt sure that in this position I would be able to minister to the emotional pain many of the women would be feeling, as well as point them back to the Lord for encouragement and renewed hope. It felt like He had pointed me to the job and opened the door wide for me. I remember driving home feeling overwhelmed with gratitude and hopeful expectation. I blasted Francesca Battistelli's "He Knows My Name" and sang at the top of my lungs.

    When she sang, "I'm not meant to just stay quiet. I'm meant to be a lion, I'll roar beyond a song with every moment that I've got." I would roar with everything I had in me; I still do, as a matter of fact. In this moment, I felt the Lord's hand heavy on me as He said, "Karen, I see you. Helping other women see themselves through my eyes, feel my love, and experience the freedom of faith in me is your purpose." It felt like I was exactly where I was supposed to be because I had walked in the shoes of many of the patients who came in for support.

I was able to minister to other women who hadn't valued themselves and their own sexuality and purity, and many who were facing an unplanned pregnancy in some way, shape, or form, just as I had. The ministry provided incredible resources and wrap-around care for the women and families facing unplanned pregnancies, as well as compassion and support for those who came to us for post-abortion medical care and counseling after being discarded by abortion clinics. Though I know it was what God had for me in that season, the commute and hours were not honoring my desire to be closer to home with my kids. So, though I do believe I was meant to be there, it was intended to be a short and powerful season.

As sure as I was that my purpose in this world was to encourage, empower, and equip other women as they walked out their own stories, life was happening. The commutes and long hours to Nashville for the job were taking a toll on me and my family. I had also been working part-time as a community-based hospice nurse practitioner on the weekends and had absolutely fallen in love with meeting patients at incredibly vulnerable times in their lives, in the most vulnerable places: their homes. It was an honor. So, when the company asked me to lead their new palliative care program, a role that would allow for a flexible schedule and to go against traffic instead of being stuck in it, I accepted.

The role allowed autonomy over my schedule and better hours. I also knew I could minister to the patients and families walking through illnesses. After all, I was hanging onto hope with everything I had in me while my healing hadn't come yet. I built relationships with my patients and their families, and our stories overlapped in ways I will carry with me forever.

I had one woman's daughter call me on a Saturday asking me to come and pray with her mother. She had transitioned to hospice a few weeks prior and they felt sure she was hanging on, waiting for something, and they thought it may be to say goodbye to me. I was in the area seeing other patients, so I stopped by and prayed over my patient. They called me thirty minutes later telling me she passed away peacefully. I had another patient who sat with me and her daughters saying, "I just want to go home." This was not uncommon, I believe we know when we are close to death and have peace about it if we know Jesus will take us home with Him. I have seen it too many times not to believe it. Her daughters were upset because she kept telling them that Jesus was coming to get her soon. They were concerned she was depressed; however, I didn't see depression. I saw someone who longed, with excitement, for what was next. I looked into her eyes and reminded her that she was still here for a reason and God would call her home when it was His time, she just had to trust Him and focus on what brought her joy, like her family. After praying together, she grabbed my hands, looked up at me with a smile, and said, "I can't wait to see you again someday." Her daughters called me about an hour later saying she was praying at her bedside and they found her peacefully passed away when they went to check on her.

God used the hospice and palliative care role to deepen my faith. I was blessed to walk with incredible people—not all knew the Lord, but they met Him through me. Not because I was in their face with my faith, but because I could feel His presence when I was with them and His heartbreak for them as I was able to minister to their pain. I bore witness to how He meets people in their long days of walking with chronic illness, as well as in their final days, and the peace that surpasses all understanding when He is in the room about to call them home. It gives me chills just writing about it.

After I had been in the field seeing patients in hospice and palliative care for about a year, I felt a stir in my spirit to go back to school. Working with patients in clinics, and now in the community, I had seen and experienced the gaps in our healthcare system and wanted to do more. Matt and I discussed the various options and agreed I would pursue a PhD in Bio-Behavioral Medicine at the University of Colorado, Denver.

I prayed diligently before I entered the PhD program. I was giving up any free time I had—time I had been using to press into the Lord and pursue Him. I clearly heard Him lead me with, "Now you need to walk in the faith I have been building in you. This will be our adventure." I trusted Him and moved forward. This would be an opportunity for me to look for and find God's hand in every detail.

The program was hybrid, meaning I was able to do most of it remotely through Zoom classes and online assignments. I traveled to Colorado once a semester during the first three years for a week-long in person intensive. I dove into palliative and community-based care research, specifically around what worked, and what didn't, to provide valuable care for patients and families. For my dissertation work, I was able to marry my full-time job seeing patients in the community with my research.

I loved everything about the PhD program, but traveling

so often and leaving my family was hard. Coordinating child care and schedules for when I was gone, and all of the other fun details of traveling, it often had the ability to be quite overwhelming—especially until I got comfortable with navigating a new city along with the campus. One morning, I remember stepping up to the security line at the airport when one of the security officers looked at me, saw the stress and sadness all over my face, and said, "Can I pray for you?" There we stood, a female security officer praying over me, a rattled mama who just left her kids, and her marriage that had a rough night, wearing a shirt that said, "I will not be shaken." Her prayer gave me the encouragement I needed to remember God was with me and the strength to tackle what was ahead of me. I gathered my two computers in my carry-on—one for completing documentation from patient visits the day before and one that housed all of my PhD work—and I made my way to the plane. I put on Lauren Daigle's album, *Look Up Child*, closed my eyes, and rested in the Lord until we landed. On that trip, I successfully passed my oral comprehensive exam and returned home as an official PhD candidate.

The next step was for me to design and complete my own study for my dissertation work. I submitted my proposal for Institutional Review Board (IRB) approval, and once approved, I partnered with a local hospital to identify patients who met the inclusion criteria for my study. I would stop by the hospital after work to complete the initial questionnaires, and then I would see them in the community to do their follow-up questionnaires thirty days later. I studied the impact of community-based palliative care on the quality of life and spiritual well-being of patients with chronic obstructive pulmonary disease (COPD). The miracle was that I completed my last questionnaire the week before everything shut down due to Covid-19; I actually think the last patient I interviewed may have had Covid. I remember having to put on personal protective equipment (PPE) to enter her room.

In the PhD program, I learned and did things that I never thought I would. I presented and spoke at conferences. I collaborated in research with other nurse scientists and was able to author and co-author peer reviewed research articles. I networked with other professionals and researchers in the medical field and became comfortable communicating with those I always considered a level or more above me in intelligence or further in their career paths. My brain was stretched as I learned quantitative and qualitative research methods, designing and implementing studies using each. I saw how research could be used to guide clinical practice. I made friends with my classmates and felt incredibly supported by my committee members.

I loved the challenge and research. Unlike during the NP program, I was in a season of life where it didn't feel like I was drowning. I found through my research that patients and their caregivers found education and spiritual support to be the most meaningful components of palliative care. That aligned with why I loved palliative care so much—those were my favorite parts, too. Any provider can do symptom management, but it takes someone who really cares to do the rest—the holistic work of addressing social determinants of health needs as well as emotional and spiritual needs.

Though the PhD program was what God led me to and was challenging in the best ways, it was also difficult. It was more difficult than I realized at the time, especially for my family. As my travel increased for work conferences and for school, Matt's schedule with UPS continued to include long days that did not allow for any family meals or having family time on weekdays. The weekends were when I would buckle down and get caught up on school work. It was a strain on our marriage, and the kids felt the absence.

We are blessed with a family that has always been willing to fill the gaps, namely, my mom, sister, sister-in-law, and my mother-in-law. One thing that made it possible for us to do all we were doing during this time was knowing that our kids felt loved and supported by them during the times that Matt and I were absent. Our kids will tell you, too, that they loved watching me pursue and achieve something great. It doesn't stop me from often wondering if it was worth it, though. If I could go back, I honestly think I wouldn't have gone back to school then. I would focus on just spending time with my kids, making memories, and supporting their hearts in the day-to-day. I can't go back, so I ask the Lord to go back into those times and places and allow them to play out according to His will and heal what needs to be healed from the times of disconnection—in all of us.

I completed my dissertation and was blessed with a promotion to a remote, work-from-home, national palliative care clinical director position just as the pandemic exploded in March of 2020. I would work from sunup to sundown with my team, building a telehealth modality and processes for our nurse practitioners to be able to access patients and provide care. Then I would brew fresh coffee, switch laptops, and work on my dissertation chapters until I couldn't keep my eyes open any longer.

Ava was a senior in high school, and her senior year

experience had been flipped upside down. Tyler was in his last year of elementary school. Though it was a tough and scary time for all, God provided what we needed in every way during that time. We had increased financial means with my promotion, the kids and I were able to be safe together at home, and though Matt was required to leave the house for his job, he enjoyed not being stuck at home and he stayed healthy.

In December 2020, I defended my dissertation virtually and officially earned my PhD and title of nurse scientist. It was the most accomplished and freeing feeling I'd had in a very long time. I was proud of myself, my husband, and my children, and I saw God's faithfulness in so many ways throughout the journey. I was filled with hope for what was next. I was immersed in palliative care research for five years as I was in the doctorate program and continued to work as a palliative care nurse practitioner in the community. As hard as it was, God blessed it as He does and uses all things for our good. I emerged as an expert in the field, and it allowed me to advance in my corporate career as new companies pursued me to lead their palliative care programs.

I believe God called me to leadership and mentorship through corporate roles, and I loved every minute of it—not to mention that God's faithfulness was on full display. Each time I was promoted to a higher position, it was when our financial needs increased. He was always one step ahead of us, providing what we needed. It was almost laughable, in a good way. I saw Him move and show up in ways that allowed me to truly lean back into Him and know that I did not have to figure everything out on my own or carry the weight of provision anymore. He was already doing it. When we pray for what we need and watch God show up faithfully, it expands our hope. I was feeling overwhelming hope in a way I hadn't ever felt before.

The biggest blessing was, after all the years of long commutes, crying in the car, and feeling guilty because I hadn't seen my babies all day—stuck in traffic and being held to the schedules set for me—I was able to work remotely. I was able to work from the comfort of my home, available to my family whenever they needed me, and being a constant presence for our dogs. It was as if all of the seeds I had sown over the years with hard work and surrender were blooming into a beautiful life in which I found peace because I consistently invited the Holy Spirit to have access to my heart. But, of course, God wasn't done. He was beginning to unfold the next lesson He needed me to learn: I was enough and valuable, even if I wasn't achieving. He made me on purpose for a purpose, and He loved me because of who I was, not because of what I was accomplishing.

Are you tired yet from reading my journey? I shake my head in awe of all that God has done in my life and all that He has allowed me to experience. I also wouldn't do it again the way I did it, ha. It was a lot. But God always reminded me that He was the leader, and I just needed to follow Him. He has always given me choices; I have always had free will, but my desire has never been to go the easy route. I want all that God has for me in this life, and I want it all to point back to Him and His faithfulness.

I have many times asked God what His plan is when I felt like I was lost in a wrong turn. One day, He said, "You're in it." I went from despair and confusion to confidence and understanding in a split second. As long as I was prayerfully taking steps and letting Him lead, I was *in* His plan—even if it felt like I was lost. I just needed to trust Him. Over the years, He has said He would bring every experience I have had together in a way that makes sense, and writing my story has helped me see it.

There were many long seasons of my life that I would "power through." I would have so much on my plate to accomplish, so many responsibilities that I truly felt like I was just surviving. I was not actually *living* my life. It was as if I believed the world around me would fall apart somehow if I got off of the hamster wheel and rested. The pushing through when I was exhausted definitely contributed to getting sick. I now know that putting my head down and powering through was another way of self harming, like the eating disorder. I was not checking in with myself to see what I needed, and I was definitely not tending to my needs. It was as if I didn't feel that I was worth caring for, and I did not know how to rest.

I don't operate like that anymore. After all, *rest* is the first thing God deemed "holy," and God also rested (Genesis 1:31-2:3). But not only that, our rest is so important to the Lord that the word *rest* is mentioned in the Bible more times than *faith, love,* or *joy*.

I physically rest because, yes, it is important, but biblical rest is more than just physical rest. What God has taught me is that I need to be able to rest in Him, in my spirit—especially when my calendar is full. I need to truly *live* my life. I need to notice and engage with those in front of me. I need to be willing to say no to adding things to my plate that steal my joy. I need to be able to release the hamster wheel way of living because it does not serve me; it depletes and debilitates me from being able to minister to others, well, from an overflow.

If you feel like you are just surviving, running on a hamster wheel of life full of responsibilities and obligations, I challenge you to lift your head, take a seat, and take a deep breath. Tell the Lord that you need Him to help you find margin. Ask Him to show you where you can make room in your life for rest, how to care for yourself, and how to rest in Him even when your calendar is full. True rest doesn't always look like physical rest, we need rest in every area to be optimally healthy and restored. That means that as believers, we are called to learn to rest and be still in our hearts, minds, and spirits—even as storms rage around us—because the Lord fights our battles.

Only God can teach us this kind of rest, and it can only be taught when we surrender and invite Him in as the teacher. Like many lessons that grow us in character, it is often a long process. I would venture to say it is lifelong. Some of the simplest verses hold the most powerful lessons: "Be still and know" (Psalm 46:10) and remind yourself "Yes, my soul, find rest in God; my hope comes from Him" (Psalm 62:5).

I pray that as you ask God to teach you to find rest in Him, no matter your circumstances, He will unravel the meaning in each of the verses and teach you how to apply them to your own life.

If you feel lost, pray that God will keep your feet bound to the paths He has laid for you, and if you are indeed on the wrong path, He will be faithful to bring you back. "Let us not become weary in doing good, for at the proper time we will reap a harvest if we do not give up" (Galatians 6:9). God knows what He is doing. Surrender all to Him and trust His lead. Your harvest is coming.

CHAPTER SIXTEEN
Lyme Disease and Deeper Healing

I had treated many patients with Lyme in my functional medicine roles; it was the dreaded illness. The symptoms and severity could range from mild to completely debilitating, and it seemed like a lifelong sentence. I had done labs to test for Lyme during that time because we always suspected it. If someone has a "mystery illness," Lyme should always be considered as an agent playing a part. But it did not show up in mine because we didn't have the sophisticated labs we have now, and the most sensitive labs we did have I certainly could not afford.

With financial stability in my corporate role and God's blessing on Matt's hard work, I was able to seek the help of a functional medicine doctor in early 2022, Dr. Michael Bernui, the one who first trained me when I graduated from the NP program. We did specialty labs that showed I had chronic Lyme disease. This meant that the flares I was having may not have been an autoimmune disorder at all, but my body responding to the infection. This was what I had been saying for years. Labs never show what you would expect to see in a patient with an autoimmune disorder. I had done every autoimmune protocol and diet out there, and though I know it didn't hurt my health, it did not stop the flares. I had also known that when I got flares, it looked like my body was fighting an infection the way God created it to. It was not attacking itself.

I know most people will say, "Well, I can't have Lyme. I have never been bitten by a tick" or "I never had the bullseye rash." The truth is, Lyme is now known to be carried by ticks, mosquitoes, fleas, semen, and more. Not to mention, the ticks that carry Lyme are often so small that people don't realize they have been bitten, and most cases of Lyme do not develop the erythema migrans, or "bull's eye" rash. Often, even if you have a strong enough immune response to attack the Lyme, it tends to stick around, hide, and stay dormant.

One place it hides is in teeth. So my theory, based on my own journey and research, is that I was exposed to Lyme as a child. Then, when I was a stressed-out, malnourished, sleep-deprived college student and had my wisdom teeth removed, the Lyme hiding in my teeth was released into my bloodstream. At that point, I was a susceptible host for an infection. My immune system was not strong enough to battle it and win. I believe I probably had Epstein-Barr Virus (EBV) around this time as well since I had been sick so often freshman year and it is incredibly common on college campuses, which further strained my immune system (when we ran labs for Lyme, we also tested for EBV which was positive for a past infection). After the wisdom tooth removal, I went on to many more years of stress that definitely suppressed my immune function. Stress alone was not the cause of my flares, but it was a contributing factor. So, of course, as our marriage stabilized and we had less financial stress, I experienced less frequent and less severe flares.

Though getting a diagnosis of Lyme and associated pathogens, like EBV and Bartonella (Lyme rarely, if ever, travels alone) was scary and surreal, it was an answer to over twenty years of prayer. I have lived most of my life never knowing when I would be sick or well. I couldn't plan trips without thinking that I might be sick. I missed mother-son kickball games because I was bedridden. I showed up to a field day covered in bruises and nodules and just pushed through because I was tired of missing out on things with my kids. And the entire time I felt ashamed, like I had not done something right or hadn't tried hard enough somehow, when I honestly did not know how I could possibly try any harder.

When I got the positive results of a chronic Lyme infection, knowing that it was a spirochete (think corkscrew) that could pass through the placenta, I scheduled labs for my children as well. Thank God I had the test scheduled because about two weeks before Ava's test, we were at a cabin where she was bit by a tick (yes, we used precautions, and I was devastated). The test was done just as her immune system was detecting it, so we were able to detect the antibodies and catch it early.

However, she was serving as a camp counselor that summer when the symptoms hit. She had very high fevers, and because we had her on antibiotics, she was vomiting throughout the day. My children have always been on the thinner side, so she looked emaciated when her very small frame lost twenty pounds in a couple of months. My sister-in-law and mother-in-law lived closer to the camp than we did, so they drove to pick Ava up, and she came home for a few weeks to rest. However, she insisted on going back to continue to serve the kids. She walked through that very difficult season like a warrior. I know how she felt because it was how I felt throughout my more than twenty-four years battling Lyme; she was not going to let it steal her life.

We both started working with Dr. Bernui on adding low-dose immune therapies to our regimens. Although Tyler was not symptomatic, his labs did show that he had been exposed, of course, so we supported his immune system as well. Ava recovered beautifully and, praise Jesus, has not had any residual Lyme symptoms. I continue to support her immune system, and she is diligent to take incredible care of her vessel.

I added ozone treatments to the already very regimented wellness routine I had been maintaining for years. I was already consistent with exercise, adequate sleep, and an anti-inflammatory diet, along with many supplements to support my detox pathways, adrenals, and immune system. There is a lot of research to support ozone-killing viruses and bacteria, and it is able to reach places outside the bloodstream. I was using my infrared sauna almost daily, which helps me detox through sweat, along with detox baths with Epsom salts, baking soda, and ozonated water. We were eating only organic foods in our home and did not use anything toxic in the way of cleaners, self-care products, etc. I also, of course, journaled and processed my emotions.

With the addition of the immune therapies and ozone treatments, the flares actually became more frequent for about a year because we were stirring up the Lyme from its hiding places and waking my immune system to recognize it (kind of like how our marriage got worse before it started healing). Lyme is a very smart pathogen and can actually hide and thrive in the body.

I believe I cleared the strain of Lyme that is associated with intermittent relapsing fevers, because when I got flares, I no longer got the fevers that would knock me down for days. *Hallelujah!* I would get nodules and the associated pain in my legs, but I could tolerate and function normally with those symptoms. However, I would have a flare after a trip that I thought might take me out.

In the fall of 2022, Matt and I celebrated our twentieth wedding anniversary at a resort in the Dominican Republic. Twenty years is a significant milestone for any marriage, but for us, as you know, it was a miracle. We had an amazing time connecting and celebrating. No responsibilities, everything was paid for ahead of time, and we didn't have a schedule. It was just the two of us being authentically ourselves. It was the honeymoon we never had. Then, on the flight home, I noticed a nodule on my leg. I took deep breaths and told my body to align with the Word of God. I showed Matt, and we prayed it wouldn't progress and would just be a very mild flare.

The day after we arrived home, I went to Dr. Bernui to receive intravenous ozone treatment thinking I could head the flare off before it got any worse. Well, the ozone did what it was supposed to do; it killed off a large load of the Lyme. When it did, the toxins were released into my system, but my drainage pathways were not prepared, especially since I had just returned from a moldy environment in the Dominican that had already created stress in my system. So, my efforts, though successful in killing some Lyme, backfired and felt like they were killing me. I had extreme fatigue and brain fog. My legs and arms looked and felt like I had been run over by a truck. The worst part was a dark feeling of depression and despair. Though flares always came with some sort of emotional consequence, such as frustration or fear, this darkness was new, and I could not shake it.

Since the labs revealed Lyme, I had been studying all that I could get my hands on to learn updated protocols for Lyme treatment. I implemented all that I had peace about doing into my own healing journey, so when this flare happened and floored me, in all honesty, I told the Lord if He was ready to take me home, I was ready. I was tired. I was frustrated. I was defeated and hopeless. I had picked up the responsibility for my healing after I had laid it down, and I could not heal myself.

But, as He does, God spoke to me, urging me to lay it back down at His feet and continue to trust and press into Him. He wanted to take me down a new path to discover the next part of my journey, spiritual and emotional healing. He introduced me to inner healing and deep forgiveness work, and I felt Him prompting me to explore my story for meaning. He also impressed upon my heart the importance of writing down everything I was discovering and that He was teaching me.

I knew that if I wanted to be equipped to truly help others, I needed to be willing to be schooled by the only teacher who truly knew the path to healing and be willing to walk through every valley along the way myself. I surrendered because I wholeheartedly trusted Him and did not have the strength, willpower, or endurance to do anything else. I had done everything I knew to do. I needed a different path, I just didn't know exactly what it was. I told the Lord I would sit in the wilderness and seek only His face as He taught me through my own healing.

The waiting was hard. I didn't get dressed many days (thank God the company I worked for did most of the meetings off-camera). I would walk around in my pajamas, crying, grieving, and crying out to the Lord while feeling things I had never felt before. I would put on my usher-in-the-Holy-Spirit-ugly-cry-song, "Oceans (Where My Feet May Fail)" when I needed to feel as close to the Lord as possible. I was exploring my story and writing everything down. It was God's appointed time to take me into the dark places I had been hiding, even from myself, to feel and heal from the trauma troubling my soul. I grieved as I reflected on the fact that I did not know how to be still, I did not know how to slow down, and because of that, I missed so much in my own life, my marriage, and being truly present for my kids. I had to dig deep with the Lord to uncover the lies I believed about myself that created coping mechanisms that no longer served me, and where they came from. He was taking me to a different level spiritually, but to get there, He would need to have access to the debris so He could clear the path, and I gave it to Him.

Eventually, the flare lifted, as they do, but the true healing work was just beginning. I have always been a patient and a practitioner who valued an integrated approach to wellness. Prayer and processing emotions had always been a part of my wellness routine, and I recommended the same for my patients. But this felt different. I invited it and told the Lord, "I don't know what to do except to run as hard and fast after You as I am able."

In my running after the Lord, I joined a Women of Faith Mastermind and coaching group that I saw advertised on social media. Normally, I would just pass by such things, as there are many, but I decided I would accept all invitations to grow spiritually. We met weekly for two hours; we were reminded of our identity in the Lord and that we had a promised life through Him. The group provided community, security, prayer warriors, and voices of encouragement when I felt defeated. I made friends that were like-minded and safe, and made a lifelong friend in the owner and President of Women of Faith, Alita Reynolds.

During this time, I decided to pick back up the pastoral counseling training I started to pursue right before I entered the PhD training and had to put it on the shelf. By the grace of God, I was allowed to start right where I left off and was able to complete a clinical pastoral licensing program, becoming an ordained minister. This was all part of how God was going to use me to help others—through counseling, just as He told me when I was sixteen years old walking out my healing from the eating disorder.

Then a friend I met at a prayer meeting told me about a Christian neuro emotional tool that had helped her heal from trauma. I wanted to be trained in the tool so I could use it in my practice, but first I wanted to experience it to be sure it was something I had peace about. It was in doing this work that I discovered that I had childhood trauma in my story that I had blocked out.

I was able to identity lies I had received and believed about myself that were still holding me captive, such as "I am not enough," "I am broken," "I am not worth protecting and no one will protect me," "It's not safe to use my voice," and "My voice doesn't matter." These lies that I believed because of the way I had been treated and what had been done to me affected every relationship I had ever had, as well as the way I perceived myself, my life, and the world around me. I was then led to do inner healing work for myself so that I could go into the hard places, the emotional wounds, and forgive, releasing myself and anyone else from the pain or shame involved.

I listened to podcasts about inner healing, watched trainings about deliverance, and went to a live inner healing and equipping session. I read anything God brought my way. I learned that even though God absolutely does continue to perform miraculous healings (I had experienced it many times over the years when flares would go immediately after prayer), often when symptoms or illnesses return, it's because there is an emotional root, or wound, that needs to be tended to. This made sense to me; I was, after all, a body, spirit, and soul. All of those parts of me were knit together in a way that worked in unity. If one component was out of sync or was dysfunctional, all the others would be affected in some way.

I did deep healing work with the Holy Spirit. I forgave others and myself. I repented for and released the lies I was believing, as well as the negative coping mechanisms I'd habituated to as a result. I replaced them with the truth of what God says about me. I was able to go to Matt and help him understand, as I now did, why my response was often to shut down or push him away when I felt scared or rejected in our marriage, and to apologize. I understood that emotional wounds that were buried alive could keep me sick, and I knew this was my time to be set free and healed in every area. It also set me on fire to help others explore their stories in order to identify where they may be stuck, why, and to work alongside the Lord to set them free.

I am not one-hundred percent well today, but I would say I am ninety percent better than I was two years ago. I continue to heal and improve daily by taking low-dose immune therapies, eating healthy, supporting my drainage pathways and immune system, and exercising and moving my body regularly. I laugh, smile, love and receive love from others. I do not take myself as seriously as I used to. I use my voice when I need to, instead of walling myself up and feeling stuck and resentful. I check in with myself to see what I need, and I stay in constant conversation with the Lord. I continue to keep my eyes on Him and don't expect myself or anyone else to be perfect. I don't entertain stress and refuse to get back on the "hamster wheel" of life, where I put my head down and power through without looking up to notice those around me, engage with my life, or allow myself to rest. I am not completely healed, but by His stripes, I know I have been, and the physical manifestation is happening more and more. Today I celebrate my healing and remain hopeful for all that God has for me and how He will allow me to help others heal.

I have seen data that ranges from three-hundred-thousand to one-million new cases of Lyme disease each year. Google it, and you'll see it's all over the place. Unfortunately, I can tell you that I believe both are low. Many people don't know they have it (raising my hand over here), and they only count reported cases. Another problem is that the standard labs for Lyme antibodies and western blots usually come back as false-negative (again, raising my hand). Rarely can you catch someone in an acute exposure; it happened in my practice only a few times. You can start antibiotics, but once it has been in the bloodstream for a while and has replicated and tunneled into organs and tissue, it becomes much more difficult to treat—*but not impossible!*

That is the message I want you to hear. Diagnoses are not your destiny. God still has the final word. Because Lyme is tricky, I do recommend working with a functional medicine provider who is Lyme-literate. The immune system must be supported, and you should avoid doing too much or too fast to overload your system. I have experienced that.

Many people, as I have mentioned, have been exposed to Lyme and have never had symptoms; this is because they have a robust and balanced immune system. It takes multiple factors to make one a susceptible host: stress, heavy metals, and gut dysbiosis to name a few. Your provider will need to understand the importance of checking for all of these. I believe our bodies were made to heal, and I don't believe sickness is God's will, so don't lose hope—even if your healing hasn't come because "The Lord sustains [us] on [our] sickbeds and restores [us] from our beds of illness" (Psalm 41:3).

If you want a very comprehensive resource on Lyme, *Why Can't I get Better? Solving the Mystery of Lyme and Chronic Disease* by Richard Schwartz, MD, is a must read; just ingest in bites. If nothing else, it will arm you with information that will help you ask the right questions of your healthcare providers. We have to educate and advocate for ourselves.

If you have been doing everything you can to heal physically but you're stuck, I recommend you start asking the Lord to reveal and heal emotional wounds you may have that are keeping you stuck. A book I highly recommend for learning how to do this inner healing type of work is called *Breaking Emotional Barriers to Healing* by Craig Miller. As you start pursuing the Lord in this area, I feel sure He will keep leading you to more resources.

It is also helpful to have someone pray with you and lead you in your inner healing sessions. I do this quite a bit with clients, and, just like breaking soul ties, it is simple yet very powerful. We are meant to feel and process our emotions. Stuffed emotions can make us sick. John 11:35 says that "Jesus wept." Jesus felt emotions, and we are supposed to imitate the life He exemplified.

Don't become one of the statistics. The CDC states that eighty-five percent of physical illnesses have an emotional root. That is *huge* and I know that is why God started teaching me more and more about emotional healing. A few great books on this subject are *Feelings Buried Alive Never Die* by Karol Truman; *Breaking Emotional Barriers to Healing: Understanding the Mind-Body Connection to Your Illness*, by Craig A. Miller; and *The Body Keeps the Score: Brain, Mind, and Body in the Healing of Trauma*, by Bessel van der Kolk.

CHAPTER SEVENTEEN
The Launch

As 2023 began, I was invited to a prayer meeting with strong spiritual warrior women. One woman, who did not know me or my story, spoke over me that God was allowing me to go into valleys to be equipped for the call He had on my life. She said I would not be called to do things as others were doing them, that it would be unique. She said God was moving me into the purpose that He had been equipping me for. She said I would set captives free, and then she ended by saying, "He says to write everything down." She had no idea I had just come through one of the darkest valleys of my life, that God told me my purpose was to *set captives free,* or that I should be writing everything down. So, when she spoke those words, hope welled in me. Her download confirmed that God was truly moving in my story.

I had known God was going to call on me to help others on a larger scale for a few years. Having worked in hospice and palliative care as a national leader and loving it, I had also been wrestling with the feeling that I wasn't doing enough in my corporate leadership roles or that it wasn't *all*

I was meant to be doing. I wrestled with whether or not I should move back into patient care and open another practice. After all, God gave me my answer; it was Lyme making me sick, and He had been teaching and equipping me to help others.

I knew I didn't want the same functional medicine practice I'd owned about ten years prior. I didn't want to manage the care of patients; I wanted them to heal and be free from emotional and spiritual wounds, as well as find physical healing. I knew that God knit us together in a way that we could not approach healing as our medical model does in the United States. And even though functional medicine is more focused on the root cause of illness than allopathic, the practitioners often don't address the emotional and spiritual components adequately, if at all. No, this call would be different.

Throughout 2023, the stirring to do more grew stronger. I took a role with a new company in mid-2022. The first six months were great, and I felt valuable. I was creating post-acute home care models to scale nationally. But the next twelve months literally felt like I had been set up on a shelf. I was confused and felt abandoned. There were things out of our control—things we had to wait on from the government—that held up the growth of the programs.

By working remotely and being forced to wait, I felt like I was alone on an island. No one was unkind; nothing was expected of me that caused me stress. It was the opposite. I had lots of free time. I felt guilty because I wasn't always busy. I would reach out to my boss to check in and see if there was anything more I could be doing; there never was. I started to feel like I didn't know who I was or what I was supposed to be doing. I was so used to being busy, to being distracted. I was used to being useful.

One day, it was like the Lord flipped a light switch inside of me and revealed that He was orchestrating all of it. He was giving me rest, and I was safe to rest. He was providing; He was teaching me I was enough even when I wasn't constantly striving to achieve and prove my worth. He was drawing me closer to Him as He brought teachers, mentors, and friends into my life who would take me to the next level in my understanding of all that Jesus allowed for when He died and released the Holy Spirit to reside in each of us.

During this time, He was setting me apart, isolating me to consecrate me for my call, while also starting to position other women around me who were walking the same path, on fire to glean all they could from the Lord, go deeper with Him, and partake in the gifts of the Holy Spirit. Once I accepted and settled into the rest He was providing, I would tell Him daily, "Okay, I am sitting down in the wilderness. I am not getting up until You tell me to. I will keep pursuing You. I will keep learning; I will keep resting and healing." So, though I was still in a wilderness season, I was at peace. I didn't need to know what was next because I knew beyond a shadow of a doubt that God knew. He was orchestrating it all, and it would happen in His time. The word He gave me for 2023 was, appropriately, *launch*. I waited patiently for the launch, which came a few days after Christmas.

The week following Christmas has always been a time of reflection for me, and this year was no different. We had sweet family time with Ava home from college. Matt and I live for the days when we have both of our kids under the same roof. Then the night after Christmas, as things settled down, dread washed over me as I thought about the new year. I sat alone on my bed with my journal in front of me and found myself in a battle with fear of the unknown. I knew God was about to strip me of everything I found comfort in outside of Him. I said to my husband one night through tears, "I feel like everything I have worked for is about to be taken away."

It took me a couple of days sitting with the Lord, processing the feelings, and preparing for the stripping before I came to the point that I couldn't stand it anymore. I was done feeling stuck. I told Him, "I need Your hand to move. I tell everyone of your faithfulness. I have seen it, I know it, and I need You to move now. I am ready, Lord." A few hours later, I had a calendar invite in my email from my boss for the following morning. My husband and friends kept saying, "You don't know what the meeting is about. Everything will be fine." But I didn't need rescue; I knew what was coming, and I needed it to happen as much as I feared it.

I woke up and got camera-ready. I called my husband, who was at work, and we prayed together. Then, with nervous sweats and a dry mouth, I met virtually with the chief operating officer and my boss. I was as emotionally and spiritually prepared as I could be. It happened just as I had seen it play out in my head. The meeting started with a few seconds of awkward chit chat and then the COO said, "I don't want to waste your time, so I'm just going to cut to the chase."

I listened as the Lord covered me with His peace and gave me the words to respond with as I heard, "Your position is being eliminated." In less than two minutes, it was done. I was no longer employed, and the security of the great income God had provided through this company was coming to an end. However, just as I felt a faintness wash over me, God, in His sovereignty and faithfulness—in His kindness to me and my family—provided severance that was more than enough.

I took a couple of days to allow the thoughts and feelings to spin and process. Remaining in the lap of the Lord, I grieved. Though I was prepared for the change that was coming, my path was unknown. And even though there were no mean words or hard feelings, I felt rejected. I had to be okay with not knowing what people were saying about me. I had to be okay with not knowing if they eliminated my position because of something I did or didn't do. I knew God had moved and this was all in accordance with His plan.

I also stood on Exodus 14:14—"The Lord will fight for you, you need only to be still"—the verse that, by this point, had my permanent footprints burrowed into it. I learned throughout my life not to waste time or energy worrying about what other people think of me. I focus on being a person of integrity and kindness, leaving my reputation to the Lord. It's not always easy, but it's near impossible to encourage others if I am always focused on myself, so I let Him fight my battles. He has always proven faithful.

After what I now call *the great launch of 2023*, I remained in the wilderness, full of great expectation of what the Lord was doing, but I was now walking instead of sitting. Cautiously and slowly, I took one step and one day at a time. I told the Lord I was willing to walk wherever He led but I would not take one step without Him. This was His plan. I didn't want mine anymore. A good friend shared a quote with me that resonated: "What God initiates, He permeates. What I initiate, I have to sustain." So, I stepped across the starting line of what was unknown and what was possible by only taking the steps that God initiated, praying that He would protect me from initiating anything that I'd have to sustain.

God had initiated this next season, and the morning after my position was eliminated, I no longer had access to emails or my calendar. I no longer had any responsibilities to anyone but God, myself, and my family. I rose with new life pumping through my veins. There would be no more distractions or barriers, just a blank page for God to continue His story for me. I felt truly free. I was not afraid because God had been speaking to me the entire year about what He was planning.

I took part in a three-week fast that my church starts each year with. Though fasts are never something I would describe as enjoyable, they have always been fruitful for me spiritually. This year, I honestly struggled more than in years past, as I felt like I was going into a time of deprivation from a deficit. I wanted to comfort eat, have a drink at night with my husband, and not think about the season I was in. It makes me laugh sometimes to see how clearly God's timing works in everything. He launched me off the cliff only when I said I was ready, though. And then He took away some of the most basic coping mechanisms, or cushions, we as humans use. I was unsettled, bored, and hungry; I was not loving it.

During the fast, the word the Lord gave me for 2024 was *pursue,* so if I was going to do this fast, I was going to milk every drop of what God had for me from it. I resolved to stay still and not look for or apply to jobs. Instead, I listened to teachings on podcasts from my church and others on YouTube. I got out books on my shelves that I hadn't had the time to read, and I journaled and prayed. There may have been more of the dressed-in-sweats-with-crying-spells-on-and-off days, but it was okay. It was all part of the process. God was still giving me rest, and I was still wrestling with it while settling into it. God set me apart to be alone with Him and was teaching me to be content in the unknown.

I was in the in-between, standing in uncertainty, and I laid my life down at the feet of Jesus because I knew there was hope on the other side of what I was walking through. If I am being honest, I hoped that there was hope on the other side of that season. I found myself constantly saying, "Lord, I believe. Help my unbelief." But God had allowed me to come to the end of myself and lay down my fears, dreams, and desires at His feet enough times that the surrender had become as natural as breathing the air He provided.

I am still in the in-between time as I write this. I have continued to learn all I can about the world of emotional and spiritual healing and trauma work—retraining my autonomic nervous system so that when emotionally triggered, my body doesn't go into a full on fight-or-flight response, resulting in my immune system bottoming out and inflammation revving up. I have worked for years to heal my adrenals, balance my hormones, and support my unique system in detoxing and remaining healthy. But through this season of advanced training with the Lord, I learned something far more important: the power and necessity of taking spiritual authority over every area of my life and doing the deep, emotional healing work. I continue to learn all that I can and pursue all that God will share with me about His kingdom truths and the power we have through Him to walk in victory.

In this season between the role elimination and severance coming to an end, God has spoken and sent me messages of encouragement, not only for myself through others but for others through me. It has been a season of going to church and knowing the message was specific to my situation or watching a preacher on YouTube who cuts right to the heart of the matter I am wrestling with. I have experienced my daily devotional aligning with other things I encounter throughout the day with the same verse. The women God was positioning around me in my isolation time have emerged as new friends who speak life into my circumstances and are prayer warriors. I have seen God equip and support me in this new season in the most unique and beautiful ways. You will find me most days walking through my home and on my treadmill, writing at my stand-up desk, roaring back as the enemy comes after me with lies and his stupid attempts at fear. I have been brought to a new level of peace and determination. In fact, Matt looked at me this morning during our coffee time and said, "I love seeing you like this. I have never seen you so determined and confident. Even though you don't know exactly what God is doing, you are so peaceful."

I know my mission; the enemy has to bow down. Through this valley, God has been equipping me to be a warrior. He has taught me how to overcome hardship by enacting my faith and the Holy Spirit's power in my life. I have realized that most of us don't understand the depths of what is available to us through the Holy Spirit. The Lord will reveal it if we ask and are willing to be teachable. The lessons aren't easy, but the rewards are life-altering for not only you but for everyone your life intersects with. My mission is to set captives free by pointing them back to their identities, power, and purpose in the Lord, resulting in renewed hope. I believe the Lord is allowing me to do that through this book.

When the fast was over, I told Matt I felt like God meant more when He said "write it down." I felt I was supposed to write a book. I have wanted to write a book since I first laid eyes on one. I love to know people's stories, and I *love* sharing stories of God's faithfulness in my life. So, I sat down one day and asked the Lord if writing a book was what I was supposed to be doing with this time.

Later that same day, I saw a post from a neighbor of mine on Facebook, Lauren Eckhardt, saying that she was releasing her memoir. I was so happy for her, and again, I thought, *I am supposed to be writing.* I looked up her website and saw that she also did writing groups and had a publishing company, Burning Soul Press. I signed up without a second thought. Lauren and I have become friends and we laugh about it now because I had so much peace and excitement about it all that I didn't even know what I signed up for; I just jumped in.

With her encouragement and guidance, and all of the time during my days free to write, I got the first draft of my memoir done in two months. I connected with the little girl in me who wanted to write and found myself in awe of the gift of time and space God had given me to be creative. I was so excited that I would often show up to the virtual writing group disheveled and sweaty because I had already walked about eight miles on my desk treadmill while writing for hours. I joked that I felt like Penny on *The Big Bang Theory* when she lost her job, and her neighbors introduced her to video games. One morning they found her, having been up all night, clothes a mess, apartment a mess, and Cheetos in her hair because she had been playing nonstop. That was how I felt. The stories were flowing out of me; I didn't want to stop. And here we are!

Ecclesiastes 3:1 says, "There is a time for everything, and a season for every activity under the heavens." Yes! God's timing really is the best. I wouldn't have been able to share my story the way I can now if I had tried to write it earlier in my life. I would not have had the understanding and heavenly perspective I now have on many things, or have been aligned with the right people to encourage and help me. I would not have had the time and brain space for my creativity to flow. You, too, are in God's plans for you as long as you are letting Him lead; it just may take a bit longer or look like a different route than you were expecting.

As Paul urged believers in 2 Corinthians 3:2-3, "You yourselves are our letter, written on our hearts, known and read by everyone. You show that you are a letter from Christ...written not with ink, but with the Spirit of the Living God, not on tablets of stone, but on tablets of human hearts."

Your story is your testimony. Your story is a letter of Jesus' faithfulness that can be used to reach the people around you. However you feel led, I pray you will share your story.

Afterword

This book was born out of the desire to share my experiences of the Lord's faithfulness with a larger audience in order to reach you and others like you. My aim was to empower, encourage, and equip; to point you back to the Lord and help you find meaning, healing, and purpose in your own story as you saw yourself reflected in mine. I hope you have had moments of revelation that you are not alone. You are not the only one walking what you're walking through, feeling what you're feeling, and thinking what you're thinking.

I won't pretend to know all that God has for me in the next chapter, but I have so much hope for what is in store. I have been blessed to be able to counsel and coach others since *the launch* and have seen the Lord show up in powerful ways. What I envision is that He will continue to use me to help others achieve wellness of body-spirit-soul through books, Bible studies, workbooks, podcasts, speaking engagements, as well as by working with them one-on-one and in groups. I have resources and programs available at www.karenhyden.com, and many more the Lord has shown

AFTERWORD

me that are in the works. I invite you to follow me @DrKarenHyden on Facebook and Instagram, and subscribe to my emails on my website to stay informed of new resources, programs, and offerings.

Because I found so much value in the therapeutic narrative process of exploring my story with the Lord, a resource I offer is an accompanying workbook for this book called *Finding Your Way Back to Hope Through Your Story* that will teach you how to plot your own life storyline with transformative events that shaped you and changed your path. Because writing your story is a powerful way to organize, reflect on, heal from, and find meaning in the events that make it up, I will start by leading you in outlining and fleshing out your story. You will highlight the times God was undeniably speaking to you, protecting you, and directing you, as well as the times you may have gotten off track because of your own decisions or things that happened to you. This process will allow you to reflect on your story from a heavenly perspective as you see the bigger picture. This includes identifying events in which there is still pain or a need for forgiveness which is an important step to make space for healing and meaning-making.

Finally, I will guide you on how to engage in the process of writing your next chapter. This is where neurogenesis happens as you meditate on verses, release lies and negative beliefs, and dream big. You will imagine your life without the chains of the past: brokenness, shame, pain, and unforgiveness.

My prayer is that as you explore your own story, you will not be like Lot's wife, who turned back and became a pillar of salt. Instead of holding regrets, shame, unforgiveness, or bitterness, my hope is that as you move through your story, you will visit painful parts of it simply to heal and find meaning. I pray you will then walk into the next chapter with inspiration, courage, and hope. If, for some reason, you find yourself feeling lost in the wilderness, take a seat and rest in the Lord, my friend. I am holding hope for you. He is making a way, and He is fighting for you.

I wish I could sit with you, curled up on a cozy couch with a soft blanket and a warm cup of coffee. Maybe there is even snow falling and a roaring fire as I listen to you share your story. I want to hold your hand as you share your heart. I want to catch your tears and feel your heartbreak, and then watch your face light up and feel chills all over my body as you share the parts about God's faithfulness and redemption that are stirring fresh hope in your spirit.

Maybe one day you will share your story with me and with the world. You are important, your story matters, and your voice has value.

Acknowledgments

I want to thank the Lord for providing the time, space, and gentle nudge to explore my story and share it with others. His faithfulness is on full display in my story.

I want to thank my husband, Matt, for his support and encouragement, and especially for his willingness to be included in the sharing of some of the painful parts of my story that involve our relationship—the parts that we have often wished we could go back and rewrite. Thank you for being scrappy with me when our marriage needed us to fight for one another. I am grateful for our love story.

I want to thank my parents for their love and support, as well as my siblings and bonus in-law family. I am beyond grateful that God made us a family and that we have been blessed to be able to continue to grow, heal, and do life together. Thank you for your unconditional love; you are my tribe, and I am proud to call you mine.

I want to thank my children, Ava and Tyler. You are the best part of me and my story. I am overcome with pride, and words can't truly express what being your mama means to me. I can't wait to see what God has planned for each of your lives. I hope you have learned what not to do from where I have stumbled. You won't be perfect, so learn to give yourself grace and seek the lessons God has for you. I pray you confidently follow the Lord and experience all He has for you. I will be your loudest cheerleader, with arms that are always open. May we have a future full of adventures, travel, and celebrations together.

I want to thank the doctors, counselors, teachers, professors, and coaches who were bold enough to speak love into my life, point me back to truth, and were bold enough to equip me with tools for identifying lies I was believing and to defeat the enemy.

I want to thank my friends throughout my life, especially Leigha and Gina. I think we have done a pretty good job of loving and supporting one another. Adulthood makes staying in touch a bit more difficult, but I know I could come to any of you and you would be there for me, and vice versa. There is something powerful about knowing I have a net of people who would catch me if ever needed.

I want to thank the warrior women God brought into my life to encourage me during the latest transition period that led to the writing of this book. Specifically, my friend and President of Women of Faith, Alita Reynolds; my friend Lauren Eckhardt, writer, owner, and CEO of Burning Soul Press; and the Burning Soul Press team, Allison and Katie.

People and relationships are at the heart of my story, and I certainly did not have the room to include all of them in this book. So, thank you to anyone who has lifted me in prayer, loved me, encouraged me, spoken truth to me, challenged me, and pointed me back to my identity in the Lord.

About the Author

Dr. Karen Hyden is a true Renaissance woman—an author, speaker, PhD-trained and double board-certified Nurse Practitioner in Women's Health and Hospice and Palliative Care, a national healthcare leader, ordained minister, and entrepreneur with a life coaching and Christian counseling practice. She is driven by her love for the Lord, her husband, two children, and her purpose—to set captives free by pointing them back to Jesus so they can encounter Him personally and find their confidence and worth through their identity in Him.

Karen has been equipped to help others through her own life experiences with trauma, an eating disorder, Lyme disease, unforeseen challenges, heartbreak, a redemptive marriage story, raising two children while completing two master's degrees and a PhD program, as well as 16 years in the medical field as a provider and leader.

Her mission is to combine her knowledge and skills with her purpose in order to encourage, empower, and equip others in their physical, spiritual, and emotional well-being so they can live the lives of joy and freedom that Jesus died for them to have.

www.KarenHyden.com

facebook.com/drkarenhyden

instagram.com/drkarenhyden

linkedin.com/in/karen-hyden-9119a127

Also from Dr. Karen Hyden

We have been knit together by the gentle, creative, powerful, and perfect hand of God, our Father—body, spirit, and soul. He knit each of us uniquely according to His plans. He has reminded me of Psalm 139:13 multiple times throughout my adult life when I felt stuck, hopeless, and off track. As He nudged me to explore, write, and share my story in this book, He showed me that He continues to knit us together throughout our lives—physically, spiritually, and emotionally—which we can see evidenced in our stories when we look back from a heavenly perspective.

I have been called to help others get unstuck by exploring their stories in the way the Lord has shown me. If you would be interested in learning more about how to explore yours or work with me, visit www.karenhyden.com for resources, services, and programs.

Made in the USA
Columbia, SC
15 May 2025